I0446404

SELLING IS NOT CHEATING

Sales is Strategy, Skills, Pricing, Marketing, and Ethics

MANOJIT MAJUMDAR

This book is dedicated to my mother, Anjali Majumdar and my wife, Debleena Majumdar, as without their help and support this journey was not possible.

I would also like to dedicate this book to all those who played an essential role in my professional journey of sales – Diwakar Nigam, Jim McCain, Jyothi Satyanathan, Mohan Joshi, Margo Robertson, Sriram Rajan, Sudhir Saxena, Hemant Kumar, Anil Menon, Satish Kaushal, and MK Bharatee.

Table Of Contents

INTRODUCTION

The objective of writing this book is to help those millions of small and mid-size businesses that have not yet reached a revenue of 100 million USD (Rs 1000 Crore). I have seen many of these organisations struggling with the basics as many businesses were set up by people who are technically strong and hence can develop good products or solutions but do not know the right way of taking them to the market. Many do not even hire a sales team, believing the need for a sales team does not exist in the initial product testing and soft launch phase.

I have spent more than 35 years in sales. It all started in college with working as a sales promotion person, going from door to door, standing in shopping areas, talking to people, and taking feedback about popular talcum powder or cigarette brands. The most thrilling experience was working weekends at the Delhi Race Club, selling tickets at the triple nomination counter. Strangely, many used to wait at my window to buy tickets as they thought I was lucky. In many cases, sales are influenced by superstition and beliefs. Datapoints do not always work.

After completing my education, I worked with multiple organisations in different parts of the country and the USA, managing branch offices or country sales operations. I worked for small start-ups like *ELX Linux* and big giants like *IBM and* attempted my own business. Now I know how naïve I was. I see a similar trend in many businesses where they work hard but do not reach anywhere. It is almost like walking on the treadmill; even after walking 10,000 steps, you remain static at the same place. People put in a lot of effort but make zero progress. So, all the things I should have known to simplify life and achieve much more with the same available resources have been written down here for easy reference. I see organisations with the potential to become billion-dollar firms struggling to reach US$100,000. Every day is a struggle for them, for they have no clue why they are struggling and unable to grow. This book is meant for them.

Sales jobs required me to travel across my home country and 40 others worldwide. I met thousands of customers and learned about hundreds of organisations during business interactions or visits to business partners, business friends and colleagues at their workplaces.

I have seen and lived the life of a salesperson for a long time, hence the desire to write this book to help people understand what they should and should not do in sales. Business depends on multiple things; however, sales and activities related to sales play a huge role in making a business successful.

When it comes to sales, the most important and common thing I found was people's stereotypical perception of a salesperson and how profoundly it impacts business. More than 10,000 MSME's[1] closed shop in 2022-23. One of the critical reasons is that they could not sell what they had. So, the question is, why the sales team could not deliver? What went wrong? Why selling an unknown brand is so difficult? How do you overcome the obstacles? The book has answered these and many other queries.

Similarly, when someone says he is a salesperson, what comes to your mind? What kind of person can this person be? The usual thought process is that this person is manipulative, talks too much, and will try to sell something, whether you need it or not. Hence, people avoid them if possible.

When customers have a negative perception, they only buy when and until they have no other option. The day they get a choice, they will go for the alternative, even by paying a higher price.

The impact of this negative perception is that it makes the selling job difficult for the frontline sales team of lesser-known brand names, even if they have not done anything wrong personally. At the same time, because organisations tend to overlook the wrong selling practices for immediate revenue, it becomes socially and professionally acceptable in most

---

[1] Staff Report, 'A Bad Year for MSMEs' *The Wire,* Feb. 8, 2023, Business Economy https://thewire.in/economy/a-bad-year-for-msmes-over-10000-closed-in-2022-23

organisations. The salesperson develops the habit of twisting facts and misrepresenting them to make selling easy. When customers start using the product, they realise that what they were sold and what they thought they were buying were two different things. They become unhappy and dissatisfied. In many cases, they stop using it or recommending it to other potential buyers. This is one of the reasons why millions of organisations cannot grow beyond a certain size and struggle to survive.

Failure to bring recurring business is not always because of poor salesmanship; there can be many reasons for it. It can be because of poor quality or unsatisfactory delivery of products or neglect in after-sales service, lack of good strategy to sell or not promoting people based on merit or something else. Do an honest review if you want to grow your business. Make serious attempt to control the negative aspects.

During COVID-19, a medical company saw a huge potential for manufacturing thermometers and pulse Oximeters. So, they quickly established a small unit to cater to this new requirement. When they got the first lot, one of the quality check employees pointed out that the equipment measurements were not always correct. The business owner himself decided to have a look. He struggled with it for some time and got the reading, which was correct. In every five attempts, it failed twice.

The owner knew that this could cause trouble but was not interested in delaying the shipment, looking at the huge demand in the market. They worked out a lower cost and shipped the material. The medical stores were desperate for materials and started stocking and selling. Soon, negative feedback started coming. The owner, however, was busy counting the inflow of money and not much bothered about the loss of business from some medical shops. He did not focus towards solving the problem.

The company had good revenue for some time and did nothing to resolve the problem. Slowly, the negative feedback started impacting sales. When their business started dropping, they blamed the medical stores, the customers and the sales team. They only started working on the product issue when the revenue came to a near standstill. The negative image impacted the sales of other products too. Meanwhile, even with a corrected system, the teams struggled to sell in the face of a longstanding negative image in the market. The company's very survival stands at risk if the trend continues.

The same is true for many other products. In many cases, 95% of the work done is excellent, but that balance of 5% becomes a showstopper. When we do not bother, it creates a vacuum for a better alternative to come and fill the gap.

The previous illustration is one of the major reasons why local competition or reputable MNCs who enter the market and charge a premium for the product or service they offer, even in a price-sensitive market, are able to sweep the market and become market leaders. We keep blaming customers that they buy anything imported and do not pay the legitimate price for a home-grown product. We refuse to accept our mistakes, hence we don't learn from our failures and the cycle continues.

We have been doing this too often and for too long. It is high time someone showed us the mirror, and without ridiculing the mirror for bad looks, let's accept and attempt to improve. This book should help small and mid-sized business houses to improve. It will help those in the leadership position look at the blind side and take necessary corrective steps.

After the second wave of COVID-19, many business organisations' problems grew, which meant business closure. Owners came under stress and, many a time, gave up on life and not just their business. As per the National Crime Records Bureau's latest report, 12,055 businesspeople committed suicide in 2021.

What compels them to take such a drastic step? Is there something wrong that we refuse to accept? We get blinded by our creation's love and refuse to look at our faults. The customers may not complain but do not come back. Businesses should learn to identify the clues they need to work on—the clues telling you to relook at your business.

Many multinationals are looking at India for high growth, which can also be seen in the rising stock market with investment from overseas. They are hugely impressed by this country's GDP growth and growing middle class. While many developed countries are heading towards near recession, India is growing. The global giants are heading towards this country to do more business.

The global heads of 10 large multibillion-dollar companies are optimistic about India and the prospect of doing business in India[2].

Tim Cook, CEO *of Apple*, says, 'India is an incredibly exciting market…there are a lot of people coming in from the middle class. I feel that India is at a tipping point.'

Alan Jope, CEO of *Unilever*, says, '*Hindustan Unilever* is the jewel in *Unilever's* crown.'

James Quincey, CEO of *The Coca-Cola Company*, says, 'India's economy remains resilient, with a strong job market and robust consumption.'

If the success of big MNCs in India is one side of the reality, the other side, as per a study by the *Economic Times*, is that 51% of the employees working in the top 24 unicorn start-ups are looking for jobs[3]. Ten out of the top 24 unicorns have laid off people since 2022. As per the *Mpower* workplace survey 2023[4], nearly 48% of corporate employees are struggling with mental health issues, with female employees at higher risk than male peers. Read the writing on the wall and take steps to control the situation.

Why are the success stories suddenly seem to be struggling? Organisations start with a dream, and somewhere down the line, the dream does not become a reality. It becomes a nightmare for many. We falter when we ignore the first few warning signals. When customers test your product

---

[2] Writankar Mukherjee and Sagar Malviya, 'India Driving Numbers for Large Consumer MNCs' The Economic Times, May 6, 2023.
[3] Rica Bhattacharya, 'For Startup Staff, it's Not All Rainbows & Unicorns' The Economic Times, May 4, 2023.
[4] Viswanath Pilia, 'Ecomm Staff More Prone to Mental Health Issues' The Economic Times, May 2023.

and don't buy it, check what you are missing. Check the product and sales strategy when customers buy once and do not return for repeat business. It could be that the sales team is not reaching out to the customers or has no promotion schemes to entice the existing users. The reason could be very basic.

When we ignore the initial warning signals, it becomes a tsunami. All our subsequent best efforts then struggle to make even a feeble mark, forget creating an impact. So, don't wait too long.

In India, growth and managing growth are big issues. Therefore, we will discuss growth first and then the other aspects. For growth, you need sales. Selling is about building trust with customers and partners. Having a good product alone will never do the magic. It would work when you have a strong sales team to sell. It is also about building the product's perceived value in the customer's mind. The customer needs to trust the company and not just the product. It helps customers make positive decisions. Trust needs to be earned.

When people see your product or read about your services again and again, they develop a liking. Become visible using social media, print media, or any other means available. This fact frequently came up in our discussions that how selling for an unknown company is such a struggle compared to working for an established global player. One simple reason was that no one knew about the product or service the lesser-known companies were selling. Building trust with the buyers was utterly dependent on the salesperson, which made creating trust even more difficult. Customers who do not trust the organisation do not like entertaining the salesperson of that organisation.

When organisations do not spend money on building a solid sales and marketing team and do not work to build brand trust, selling becomes difficult, and dependence on individual skills and connections becomes more important. Individual connections help only to a point, as any individual will have limited reach in the needed set of potential customer organisations. Secondly, if the person decides to quit and go, the business starts slowing down. Hence, depending on one or two persons with personal charisma is not a good strategy. It can be a starting point but not a strategy to drive revenue.

You need a good sales strategy to grow your business.

Many entrepreneurs start a business without working on the sales plan first. To succeed in sales, your team needs a complete support system. The organisation's culture, the product's quality, the need for the product in the marketplace, the marketing support, the distribution network, the vision of the organisation, and many more things impact sales. So, do not think of sales in isolation. Think of it as a part of the body, and a body part will only function effectively when the overall body is healthy and in good shape.

In the upcoming chapters, we'll delve deeper into the sales world vis-à-vis all the facts and issues that plague it. This book will provide practical strategies and guidance for achieving sustainable growth.

Let's discuss sales.

1

CHAPTER

Why Selling is Not About Blabbering

Selling does not mean blabbering unnecessarily to win some debate. The concept of selling a comb to a bald man is a bad example. Selling means solving a customer's problem for which they would be willing to spend money and not selling a dream they know can never be true. The desire to become an instant success or to achieve success at any cost is the kind of thought process that makes salespeople commit things they should not. Getting customer acceptance takes time and needs an investment of patience. So stop pushing your sales teams to sell by hook or crook.

Need for customer support and acceptance

If you are selling a product that needs your technical support or help desk team's assistance to make it work every time, you have work to do .

Organisations get into business believing that what they are selling will have a considerable market demand based on the global demand for such products and solutions. Consequently, since in some way, their offering is unique, they will have a definite advantage. They believe that the primary thing they need to work on is lower pricing, or in some cases, their superior craftsmanship will help them get a premium. Such innocent thoughts can be disturbing. They join the market with much confidence, and then reality hits them when they don't sell enough to survive the first few years. The brave ones with deep pockets do hang on, hoping for a revival.

There are 2,75,000 registered mid-sized and small enterprises in India with a revenue of US $1 million to US $30 million, and they have the potential to grow provided they can create a blueprint of growth. One of the important factors is the perception they create about their product. A positive perception is very important.

The importance of perceived value

Let us take the example of the stent market for heart patients and the artificial skin market for burn patients to understand the impact of perceived value in sales and how it impacts your business.

In a discussion with a senior doctor, it was revealed that heart patients are more accepting of stents. In contrast, burn patients often hesitate to opt for synthetic skin alternatives. This is when both situations have a significant impact on patients' lives. Heart patients with a blockage go for a stent without thinking much. They rarely explore other options, and in most cases, they do not even go for a second test in a different hospital to check if the first diagnosis was correct.

Whereas severe burns can cause emotional distress and affect job prospects, leading to long-term consequences, most customers still do not opt for artificial skin. The willingness to buy synthetic skin replacements is comparatively less to that of stents. Out of 4,50,000 burn cases, around 1,40,000 patients face severe deformities due to burns, significantly impacting their lives.

Skin replacement alternatives are not popularly known, and even when they are told to the patients, most choose not to go for it. One reason is that burn cases are more common in poor neighbourhoods, which do not see much value in getting the replacement. They would rather live with the scar than incur the high cost.

On one hand, 30% of stents are implanted unnecessarily because the patients believe they need the implant. The fear of losing their life makes them make that decision. On the other hand, many burn patients don't consider the skin alternative a survival necessity, even though it could significantly improve their quality of life and livelihood.

This explains the importance of the perceived value of any product or service and the demography will guide the buying decision of any product.

Usually, people from the upper middle class and upwards face heart blockage problems. They have the financial capacity to buy stents. The perception that by not having a stent implanted, they can lose their life forces the customer to decide in favour of purchasing the product, even when they may not need one. In contrast, people from the lower middle classes usually have burn accidents. For them, buying a skin alternative is not a priority; hence, they usually do not buy the product even though it often impacts their livelihood. So, the learning from this is that even if the product or service you sell has got immense value, it may not sell if the perceived value in the eye of the potential customer does not exist.

The Second step in the sales journey is understanding how to position the product. Why will a customer buy your product?

To ensure customers start buying your product, define the buying process for every product or solution you intend to sell and map it with the selling process.

Aligning the buying and selling process

The buying and selling processes are two sides of the same coin. When a customer buys a product or service, the buying process involves the steps they go through, but the selling process involves the steps a seller takes to sell their product or service successfully. Every organisation should map the sales process to understand how to approach the market to make the sale happen.

1. Budget

Buying process: The customer defines a budget that it will use to buy a given solution. They usually do this by looking at the available options and how they satisfy their need for a given product or solution. They may even compromise on features or quality when on a low budget. In such a scenario, products above the customer's paying capacity will struggle to get acceptance.

Selling Process: The seller identifies the market segment and the potential customers who can buy the product. They consider the use of the solution and define the price at which it would like to make the sale happen. If their pricing is higher, they should either approach a higher market segment with more buying capacity or create a good storyline to support that extra cost that customers must incur. If your pricing strategy is not in sync with the customer's capacity to pay, the product may never succeed.

2. Acceptance of Solution

Buying process: The customer will evaluate multiple solutions and try to reach a conclusion on the probable and most reasonable solution it can procure based on the requirement. They may like to use the product to see its suitability. They may talk to other users to verify if they are considering the right product.

Selling Process: The seller should ensure that the product will work as expected when the customers independently verify it. Alternatively, the product demonstration should always happen in the seller's premises where someone can assist the customer. Customer testimonials should be available to win customer confidence. Look for the wow factor in your product or solution and ensure that it gets highlighted.

3. Need

Buying process: The customer evaluates the need for a product based on urgency. If the need does not seem strong, they can defer the purchase, which can be the reason for the delay in decision-making.

Selling Process: The seller should identify and highlight the compelling reason for the customer to act and make the purchase. If the need does not exist, try creating one. One may have to highlight how things will improve after the procurement of the product or solution. Customers do not always know about the availability of products and how they can help. Hence, the sales teams have to help them understand. Someone would have explained the need for cutlery before people started using it.

4. Timeline

Buying process: Customers determine the timeline for acquiring a product based on their needs, budgets, and internal pressures. Many internal and external factors can impact this.

Selling Process: The seller needs to ensure a storyline to help the customer decide within the defined timeline. It should also help the customer understand what they can potentially lose if they do not decide now. Identify the influencers who can help the customer take a positive decision and work with them.

It's important to note that the buying and selling processes are interconnected. Sellers must continuously adapt their strategies to align with customer needs and preferences, often creating a need that never existed. For example, until Apple came out with an iPhone without a physical keyboard, no one wanted something like that because they could not even imagine that something like that was possible and would be acceptable to the customers. iPhone created the need, and the rest is history. People do not always make decisions based on facts and figures. Hence it is not necessary that the market leader will always win against an unknown product. So, one of the reasons people buy a product is because the decision maker likes the product, even when others may have a different opinion.

Key growth influencers

Every business has its challenges and reasons for success or failure. Here, we have identified a few factors that impact the growth of organisations. Please create a checklist, see what issues plague your organisation, and work to resolve them before it is too late.

Hiring:

Many organisations fail to prioritise the hiring of sales teams. They do not hire the required number of sales and marketing team members who fit the role perfectly. They do not create the needed structure and systems to drive that structure and expect sales to happen. They make a wrong start and usually pay a price for that.

Experience and exposure are two critical factors in determining a person's ability to deliver. If the job involves meeting senior people in big organisations, you must also hire senior people in your team. When you have to face a lion, do not hire rabbits to negotiate just because they are economical to hire.

Hiring quality manpower is important. Quick learners and those ready to experiment can be game changers. The quality of the people you hire will decide your organisation's future; hence, be very careful to ensure you have the right mix of high and mediocre performers. There are job profiles where you need people who will follow instructions and do exactly what is expected, and there will be a need for people who will use their own minds and innovate to come out with smarter ways of handling sales and marketing. Have a healthy mix.

Introducing a new product line or a new growth approach requires unlearning old methods and then retraining the mind for new sales and marketing methods. Many will find it difficult to switch and adjust to changing systems and processes. They can become the real bottleneck for the growth of the organisation.

Finally, in India, hiring is very focused on educational qualifications. However, Rabindranath Tagore, the first noble laureate, did not go to any school or college for formal education. Going by the hiring preferences, he would not have had any job in this country. So, you should hire based on the potential to deliver and not just on mark sheets.

Training:

In the recent past, five individuals had to be admitted to a hospital because they were served dry ice instead of mouth freshener. It was a mistake, a terrible mistake which led to blood vomiting. This happened because the employees were not trained enough to understand the consequences of mixing these two things. A small training problem which caused them their business. That is the value of training.

There is a saying in the army: the more you sweat in peacetime, the less you bleed in wartime. It is true in business as well.

One of the primary challenges that new businesses with an excellent product line face is the lack of adequate training. The sales team is not trained to articulate the product or understand the customer's issues and concerns in using the product. As a result, the adoption becomes slow.

Customers need to understand how the product can solve their pain points or enhance their lives in a way that existing alternatives cannot. Without a clear value proposition, customers may not grasp the relevance or significance of the product and may be hesitant to try it. This needs regular training of your sales team. Mock calls, role plays, and anything else that can prepare your sales team to handle the customer objections better should be done to get them ready to sell.

Organisations often operate with teams that lack the necessary pitching skills, leaving them ill-equipped to withstand the challenges established competitors pose. This is one big reason for a long sales cycle and losing out when faced with more popular competition, even if your product is more suitable.

Building customer trust: Understanding the challenges your customers will face while deciding on the product to buy and helping them with facts and figures to choose from will help build trust.

In 1987, when I joined the IT industry as a salesperson selling IBM-compatible personal computers, we faced resistance. People were afraid of automation. Employees thought they would lose their jobs, and the business owners believed that the cost of buying the hardware, training people, etc. would become an additional burden, and many opted out.

So, this needed building trust and confidence among the customers, which was not easy. Many business houses believed that once they get computerised, they would not be able to hide their books of accounts from people with whom they do not want to share the exact details. They saw the personal computer and the software along with it as a problem and not as a solution. Salespeople and sales organisations helped potential customers see value in purchasing a personal computer and helped them overcome their fears. Sales teams needed regular training to make this happen. Organisations which did not train their sales teams had to shut down their business.

Reduce dependency on few key customers: Small organisations have a few key customers or clients contributing a significant portion of the revenue. Losing one major customer can substantially impact revenue and overall business viability. Maintaining healthy cash flow also becomes a challenge. In such cases, seeing the dream company go down the drain takes little time. Adding new customers on a regular basis, irrespective of their size and potential for future business, is extremely important. Some of them can give you business in the future, too.

Diversification of customers: Focus on having a diversified customer base from the beginning, which is difficult but necessary. It can help spread the risk and be less vulnerable to fluctuations in any customer segment.

A diverse customer base can help businesses offer various products or services that appeal to different demographics and increase their market reach.

Newgen Software started by selling to Banks, and they concentrated on that. On more than one occasion, they found a need for an Accounts Payable solution from some of their customers. They worked with the customers, learned about it, and then created and implemented the solution. This opened opportunity in many Enterprises where they wanted to implement an Accounts Payable solution. This helped them go beyond Banking. Today, they have a diversified portfolio and hence can work with non-banking customers in different market segments, helping them grow their business.

Once a company reaches a certain size, it can either refocus on one large industry segment or continue to maintain multiple focuses. Keep evaluating your options based on the ground reality prevalent at that point of time.

Building redundancy: Build redundancy in the system to avoid surprises. Building redundancy does not mean giving two persons the exact job profile. A complementary job profile helps better control business, as it gives you a broader view of the business, and one person's job profile can be extended to manage the other person's work if needed for a short duration. This is very relevant for small and mid-sized organisations where manpower turnover is quite high. One resignation by a salesperson creates a vacuum impacting business. This method will reduce the impact on business.

Let us take an example to understand this. If you have a sales territory like India managed by 5 Salespeople, have one channel salesperson working with partners on the same accounts. The Channel salesperson's job is not to drive new business but to leverage the partner's network across the country and ensure their presence in the accounts the sales team is driving. Now, if a salesperson decides to quit and go, the partner can continue with the relationship and get help from the channel resource to pursue the opportunity until the new salesperson joins the team. This will allow the organisation to manage more accounts with the same resources. This will also ensure that you will not lose business because of attrition in the sales team. The channel works like a net, which will not allow opportunities to slip easily. It also becomes like the internal auditor, who will give his own report on opportunities and their progress based on the feedback from the partners.

Lack of systems and processes: Systems ensure that people work the way the leadership desires. It creates a structured framework for sustainable growth and long-term success. This reduces confusion and reduces the chances of blunders being committed by the sales team.

Let's take an example of a new start-up in the enterprise product business, say ABC Software. They hire two junior salespeople to help with sales. The salespersons go out for meetings with customers and return with new customer requests. In many meetings, the customer promises to place an order provided he gets a few things added to the existing software at the same cost. The owner tried explaining the financial implications of this. He explained that if all the asks of customers were to be met, then Maruti Alto would become Mercedes. The cost of production would be so high that they would not survive to run the business. Hence, he wanted the sales team to focus on selling what the organisation does have.

The sales team was struggling to sell, so in desperation, the organisation agreed to a case with a lot of commitments which were difficult to deliver at the same time and price, but they went ahead and picked the order. The customer was promising a long-term association. In addition to this, they could become a reference for future sales. It looked like a risk worth taking. Rahul, the owner of the firm, agreed. Halfway through the project, the customer asked for a few extra changes in the specifications, as some of the essential people in the customer's organisation got involved quite late in the discussion. The sales team again agreed. The design and development team started getting jittery. They were worried that some of the things being committed may not be possible to develop and deliver. What they were now trying to deliver was much more complex and different from what they were prepared for.

Under pressure from his delivery team, Rahul approaches the customer to reduce their new ask. He told them they could do some things as per the new ask, but not all. The customer got annoyed, threatened to sue them, and stopped all payments.

Rahul finally realised they should not have agreed to so many changes in the first place. Maybe he should have trained his team better to handle customer objections. Maybe he needed people with more experience to handle enterprise sales. He should have clearly defined the systems and processes to avoid making wrong commitments. Overcommitments are common under three circumstances. The first is when your team is not skilled enough to handle objections; second, when the pressure to perform exceeds the team's capability to deliver; and third, when the product is not good enough. Proper planning and strategizing can help.

Wrong commitments can kill your business: There are consequences when you make commitments that the organisation cannot honour. You can lose all future business and struggle to get your payments. Negative news spreads fast and impacts your chances of doing business with other customers. When Rahul walked out of the client meeting, his head was spinning at 3000 revolutions per second. He was unsure if he should continue the business or shut it down and search for a job. The half an hour journey back to the office seemed really long.

Hopefully, Rahul learned an important lesson that selling is not about blabbering and winning debates. It is about understanding customer problems, providing a solution with the limitations in mind, and building trust. Instead of agreeing to every ask of the customer, they should have explained to the customer better the constraints and challenges of changing specifications midway. No product will be hundred per cent perfect, but still, many help create a billion-dollar organisation. Let's discuss how.

2
CHAPTER

The World of Sales

It was summertime in the 90s when a salesperson visited the *Hartron* office in Mohali. This office was responsible for automation in the Haryana government, and hence, anyone who wanted to sell computers or software to the government of Haryana used to visit *Hartron*. The salesperson walks into the office to meet a senior person there. He was slightly sweating. He wiped his face, combed his hair, and approached the officer concerned.

The salesperson wished good afternoon to the government official sitting at the desk. The government official promptly asked if he was there to sell something. The salesperson was a bit surprised and enquired, 'Sir, how did you know that I am a salesperson?'

The official replied, 'Only salespeople move around in the sweltering heat of 45 degrees centigrade in North India. Even the street dogs look for shade or a place to hide at this time of the year and day!'

The salesperson was taken aback as he had not been expecting this.

Managing unpleasant experiences under trying circumstances is part of the unwritten job profile. Prepare your sales team to manage difficult situations. You do not want them to give up, so keep them motivated.

Approaching the marketplace
Organisations need to strategise and decide their approach to address the market. They can go to the market using their own sales team or have a combination of their own sales team and partners or dealers. One can even leverage third-party organisations that provide salespeople on a contract basis. Salespeople on contract are useful when you are not sure if you would like to maintain them in the long run. They help in keeping the running cost

under check. The decision between an in-house team, contractual resources or leveraging partners depends on various factors, such as the nature of the product or service, target market, scalability requirements, and available resources. This is an important decision; hence, ensure that whatever you decide, you follow that wholeheartedly. Create a strategy around the approach to ensure success in the marketplace.

Differentiating between product sales and service sales:

Customers' needs and preferences often decide how products and services are sold. By understanding these differences, the right audience can be identified and targeted. The sales approach for products versus services can vary significantly. In the case of products, one may need to demonstrate the product showcasing the functionalities, whereas, in the case of services, the availability of skilled resources and expertise in that field may become more important for trust-building. Developing effective sales strategies requires understanding these nuances.

Tangibility: Products are tangible goods that customers can touch, feel, and see. Examples include smartphones, clothing, and furniture. In contrast, services are intangible offerings such as consulting, software programming, or accounting.

Ownership: In the case of products, the customer owns them outright and can use them as they wish. When customers purchase services, they buy the service provider's expertise, time, labour or solution for a defined time period.

Production and Inventory: To ensure product availability, manufacturing or procurement processes are required, which may involve inventory management. Services are usually produced and delivered on demand without physical inventory.

Customisation: Products can be standardised or customised to some extent, but customisation options may be limited compared to services. Services are often highly customisable to meet individual customer needs and preferences except for SaaS-based solutions as they are products offered as a service for a defined time period. In SaaS you use the internet to deliver the solution and the sales process is quite similar to that of selling a software product as you are allowed to use the product of your choice at a given price for a defined time period.

Consumption: Products are typically consumed immediately or over time after purchase. Services are consumed as they are delivered, often in real-time or over a period agreed upon by the customer and the service provider.

Production costs, market demand, and competition often determine a product's price. Several factors may influence service pricing, including time, expertise, complexity, and perceived value.

Marketing and Sales Approach: Product marketing often focuses on features, benefits, and tangible attributes. Service marketing may emphasise expertise, customer satisfaction, trust, and intangible benefits.

Understanding the difference between selling products, services, or both can help tailor effective sales and marketing strategies.

Organisations have started commoditising services and have packaged the offering like a product so that selling and buying become easy.

This means that if the services business is to deliver people with *SAP* implementation experience or *Oracle* implementation experience, it is more like a commodity sale. Similarly, even the service of a plumber or electrician can be sold like a commodity. What you need is the availability of skilled people with specific functionalities or products that have an existing need in the marketplace.

The challenge of the commoditising services business is that the entry barrier gets reduced in some cases. The Indian IT industry is a classic example of this kind of services business. IT companies provide skilled software professionals for a given fee on a time and material basis. However, as it is easy to hire skilled people and start a services business, you have a lot of new entrants every year. One can bring value and differentiate themselves by bringing superior project management skills and assigning the right people for the job.

Working with the partner ecosystem

An organisation can have multiple types of partners. Depending on the line of business one is in and the stage of the growth cycle they are in, organisations can define their strategy for partners and approach them for a tie-up. To succeed in nurturing this relationship, one needs to define the objective of the relationship and create a focused team to work on the relationship. Vague objectives usually do not work; hence, be specific. For example, we should do 10% of our business through partners in the next three years, which can be the objective. The next step will be to define how you will achieve that. For that, define the team's KRA and align the other teams' activities accordingly. For example, define the market segment where the partners will operate, the marketing and post-sales support that will be extended, the geographies you will cover leveraging the network, and how conflicts will be resolved. These are basics without which the system will struggle to deliver.

Resellers: These are the partners primarily responsible for buying and selling the products without adding value. However, some do call them value-added resellers.

Independent Solution Vendors: They are partners who can take the product from the principal and build a solution on top of the product. So when they sell the solution to the end customer, the product gets sold, too. One can even use the skills of such partners to create solutions for different verticals based on their strengths. Once you see traction in that vertical, one can add that vertical as part of the focussed vertical for the organisation.

Distributors: They partner with product companies, handle their distribution in a given geography, and are responsible for creating a partner network or supporting the existing partner network, managing sales and collections through the partner, and helping the product company manage sales better. However, this does not mean that you can offload your sales responsibilities to a Distributor. Distributors can help but cannot replace your sales team.

Strategic Partners: Partners who may not be resellers but have skills and technology that can be leveraged for selling in the market. They can be big global giants or mid-size organisations with specific technology or skill sets.

Global System Integrators: Usually, this term is common in the IT industry, used for organisations that operate globally and offer solutions to end customers by becoming the aggregator of different products which will go in a solution and stitch the deal which will work for the end customer.

Regional System Integrators: They are solution providers who work at a regional level, help procure products from different vendors, and provide the solution to the end customer.

Services Partner: Partners specialising in offering services on top of a given product line are known as service partners. They build a team of skilled people for this, usually have less sales capability, and are dependent on the principal for business. They offer services at a lower cost and make the product offering economical for a customer.

Consulting partners: Accenture, KPMG, Deloitte, and McKinsey can be classified as consulting partners. Many smaller versions of these partners can also be effective and helpful in acquiring new customers or dealing with existing customers.

One can work with small partners with limited infrastructure and manpower support or big global partners. Signing up with smaller partners is usually easier as they are more accessible, but making them commit people and resources to drive business is challenging. Their dependence on you will be higher in the initial phase. However, once they start earning revenue and a substantial part of their revenue generation from your product line, they will start operating independently. They will be able to contribute much more.

Every organisation should know and understand how to strike a balance between different types of partners. Things usually do not work out in a one-sided relationship where one partner sees value and not the other. Hence, the golden rule of forming alliances is to focus on that segment of partners who see value in working with you. This will ensure that your team will not struggle to understand how to get value out of the relationship, as both teams will put in equal effort to grow the business.

Partners would like to see your presence on the ground and the potential to make big money while working with you. You have to sell the dream and prove that the dream is achievable. This might mean a lot of initial effort by your team, irrespective of the type of partner you sign up with. More significant partners will need bigger financial earning possibilities.

The success of the partner selling your product line is the biggest success factor one should chase. This will ensure that your business grows and partners show interest in working with your organisation.

In *Newgen Software*, my colleague Jagdeep and I from the Channel Sales team travelled to Mongolia to explore the possibility of doing business with the big banks and big enterprises there. We identified the potential partners we can leverage to do business. We found Infosys's presence in one of the banks. We did all the hard work and then involved Infosys in routing the deal through them, as they were the bank's trusted vendor. The selling became easier. In the process, Infosys made money; we managed to sell our product, and the customer was happy that they got the solution and one of their trusted partners was in the deal. It was a win-win for all.

So, when trying to enter a new market or segment, spend the time and effort identifying those who can help you and consider collaborating with them.

Most successful partners may not be interested in working with a less-known organisation. There are several reasons why they may not always be interested in association with less-known companies or products:

1. Risk: Working with less-known products or companies can be seen as riskier due to uncertainties regarding their market viability, scalability, and potential returns.

2. Resource Allocation & Brand Image: Successful partners, big or small, get requests from multiple vendors to work with them. Even after signing up, the sales team of the partners may not show any interest in taking it forward if they do not see the market pull. If no resource or team gets allocated to sell the product, chances are no sales will happen even after a formal tie-up.

3. Economies of Scale: If they are not selling enough of a given product, it becomes less attractive financially. In such a case, they will only take it up when they get an opportunity. No sales effort can mean no sales ever.

4. Regulatory and Legal Considerations: Operating in multiple countries entails navigating complex regulatory and legal environments. Partners may hesitate to engage with less-known players due to concerns about compliance, liability, and legal risks. The constant question that haunts them is what will happen if they encounter a severe business issue with a customer, more so in the developed marketplace, where the penalty for failure is high. Will the unknown company be able to support them in coming out of the legal issue?

Brands and products with less-known names need to focus on several key strategies to gain the attention of successful partner communities.

1. Demonstrate Unique Value Proposition: Clearly articulate what makes your product or brand unique and valuable. Highlighting features, benefits, or innovations that differentiate you from competitors can attract partners' attention, helping establish credibility and trust.

2. Viability: Provide market research, customer feedback, and sales data to prove the market's potential. Sell your product to the potential partner or global giant in the way you would sell it to a customer. This will include mapping the partner and understanding their internal structure, the teams

who can see value in working with you and the people who can be your influencers inside the organisation.

3. Invest in Branding: Invest in branding so your product becomes more known in the market segment where you wish to operate. Developing a brand story and effective marketing campaigns, including participating in trade events, social media campaigns, webinars, etc., would help. Ensure they notice the effort you are putting in to gain visibility. Talking about the investment in branding is as important as the investment itself, especially when operating out of a shoestring budget.

4. Focus on Scalability and Growth Potential: Run with them in the marketplace and show them the possibility of high growth by helping them engage with multiple customers. This can glue them to your product line instead of competition.

5. Help them stay competitive: As you are small and agile, you can adapt more to the changing market needs. Identify areas where your agility in the marketplace can help; demonstrate the same whenever you can.

6. Your presence on their premises: Find a reason to sit and work with their sales teams, be present in their sales office, and motivate their sales teams to promote your product. This approach always works.

7. One recommended method is to jointly develop a solution with your partners and go for a joint "Go To Market". Clearly define the ownership and responsibilities. Monitor the outcome at regular intervals. This is one effective way of leveraging each other's strengths to do business.

The initial journey with partners can sometimes be time-consuming, exhausting, and discouraging. However, once the model starts working, one can see the vast difference in revenue versus the expense incurred for that revenue.

So, the learning is that you should not completely depend on your partner alone to create the pull for your product. This will never work. You should do everything you will if you want the sales to happen, except that the partners do that part of the work, which you could do with extra resources and funding. Think of the partner as an extended arm. Ensure they see success working with you. This will increase loyalty and increase your ability to grow your business, keeping exponential expenses under check.

Many organisations working with big giants in their respective businesses collapse for reasons that can be slightly complex to understand initially. Nonetheless, you do not want to be on that list.

For example, the agreement can be that you must pay them 100% in advance and get your payments when the customer pays. If you are not good at controlling the end customer, you may lose out financially, risking financial loss and closure in some cases.

Look at the bigger picture, weigh your options, and then decide. Sometimes, all this work, which looks lucrative from a distance, can bog you down and divert your manpower, finances and focus in a direction that may not be worthwhile. However, at the same time, similar kinds of partnerships have helped organisations grow big and have helped them increase their reach, too, so evaluate all the possible angles from your organisation's perspective before you decide to go for the execution of the plan or drop the plan.

BPASS is a *Newgen* partner in North India. They quickly picked the software and delivery skills on the product line. They got a team trained. This meant a lot of running expenses for *BPASS*. In every deal, *BPAAS* had to pay the license cost in advance. *Newgen* did help them get the payment released from the customer and also helped them win new deals in their service business through the Partner Support Centre. It worked very well for them, and in less than three years, they had built a 100-person team and are running a profitable business. *Newgen* is also assisting them to enter different geographies.

Building the ecosystem and gaining the trust of the partners is difficult work. You have to make sure that they succeed and make money. If the partner loses trust because they cannot sell, they will stop promoting your product.

Direct Sales

When focusing on direct sales, the primary goal is to sell products or services directly to the end customer without any middlemen. Direct sales give businesses complete control over how their brand is presented to customers. This ensures consistency in messaging and branding, which can enhance brand recognition and customer loyalty.

Businesses can retain a larger portion of the revenue that would otherwise be shared with intermediaries when selling directly to customers. This is, however, a more expensive way of approaching the market; hence, many organisations use a mixed approach of direct sales teams and channel partners or dealer teams.

Direct sales allow organisations to build direct relationships with customers, and this helps them understand customer issues and concerns much better and facilitates faster reaction time. This also helps create a customer database that the organisation can use exclusively, and personalised campaigns can be run.

Selling online

Amazon, Flipkart and similar e-commerce portals are familiar places for people to list their products. Listing your product there is just the first step. Just listing them on *Amazon* or *Flipkart* or creating your web portal to sell products online will not guarantee sales. You have to create the needed visibility among the potential end users. There are different methods of becoming visible in such portals, and some of them have been discussed in the chapter "make some noise and become visible". All these portals also allow you to promote your products through keywords, good reviews, videos explaining the product and marketing campaigns. Many of these things need common sense and hard work; some need a budget.

You can leverage your partner network to sell them online, too. Work on a model to recognise the partner's effort and reward them. Look at the Salesforce or Amazon Web Services business model, which primarily sells online. They have a huge partner network to sell. Even for an online business model, you need feet on the street. Boots on the ground are mandatory to win any war.

Signing up with big or small partners is not a ticket to success. You have to create the needed pull for your product and ensure that the partner's sales team trust your organisation and your product to achieve success in sales. So, working with the team engaged with customers regularly is mandatory. Win their trust to win the market. Trust is like an invisible currency, very hard to earn and very easy to lose. If your team has made a mistake, do not avoid talking to the partners to resolve the issues as soon as possible. Mistakes, however trivial, can start impacting the relationship and will impact business.

Establish a relationship based on trust

Many mid-size organisations fail to take advantage of the dealer or partner network. One primary reason is the lack of trust between them. The partner is afraid that the principal will sell directly and not pay the margin to the partner, and similarly, the principal of the product has his own set of reasons for not believing the partner network. The result is poor business. Create systems and processes that are easy to understand and follow. Ensure that the interests of both parties are taken care of and follow the system with minimal or no exceptions.

How the Wrong Sales Strategy Can Kill Your Business

A sales strategy is essential; having the right one is even more critical. Competitors can and do swiftly capitalise on any gaps or opportunities arising from gaps in your product or service. Work closely with your partners and customers to understand the mismatch in expectations and delivery. The business risks losing its hard-earned market share to rivals for not listening to its partners and customers.

Many of us have no strategy to hold on to the existing market share. Customers do not always change vendors for a cheaper option. The process of going away starts with a very small thing. It can be a lack of response, a lack of desire to engage with the customer for the problems raised or a lack of desire to look at a new business model to manage the changed dynamics in the marketplace.

A Gurgaon-based organisation started offering online personal computer support services with the help of their 2000-plus support executives working round the clock. They helped customers update their anti-virus and office productivity software or fix any basic-level operating system problem remotely. The customer was happy, and the business was growing rapidly. Afterwards, it was revealed that some support executives had misused customer information. In addition, the staff complained about the quality of the tools they used, as they were not helping them do their job efficiently.

Their partner in the US started complaining of poor support from the Head Office. The news spread fast, and legal cases were filed. The investors got scared and wanted to pull out. Signing new customers became problematic, and the flourishing business started going down. After running a successful business for seven to eight years, they shut down by the end of the 11th year. It was such a sad end to a budding business.

Systems and processes to monitor how your team deals with customers are very important. An independent feedback system that helps you know what your customers think about your product and service is also extremely important. Look for warning signs and act on them without delay. A small problem can become a big nuisance if not managed immediately.

Selling is not Manipulating
On closely observing the big giants and their successful track record, one thing is apparent: selling does not mean cheating. However, when some of them try to cheat, they pay the price. So, as an organisation, if you believe that selling is manipulating customers and partners, kindly take a step back and think again. Would you like to buy from an organisation that does not believe in ethics? Would you like to buy a product or service that does not work as you were told? Until and unless you do not have any option, you will never go to such an organisation. So why do you think someone else will do that?

Ensure that you deliver what you promise. Stop cheating in the sales process by lying about your product or service or harassing your customers in after-sales service. Focus on quality and honouring commitments, and growth will follow. A cheated customer is a bad reference, which is never good for business.

Gain customer trust

Salespeople can come from various backgrounds and have different personalities, skill sets, and motivations. Some may use manipulative tactics to increase business, while others prioritise building genuine customer relationships and understanding their needs before recommending a product or service.

Organisations must believe in the philosophy of building genuine customer relationships and should discourage manipulation. Many organisations do not understand this concept well and think that sales cannot be done without manipulation, resulting in distrust and unhappiness. We need repeat and reference customers to reduce our promotion expenses and increase sales. Hence, the organisation must define the ground rules for engaging with customers, and everyone must follow them.

Selling requires building trust with the customer. When the customer trusts the organisation, the desire to buy becomes stronger. This does not necessarily mean a sale will happen; it means that the customer will be willing to explore.

Managing opportunities

Assuming that your organisation is not a big brand name and has a problem getting business leads for closure, every lead is important, and you need to prepare your team for every opportunity the salesperson gets. Even in online business, the landing page or the portal where the customer will have the opportunity to know about your product or service will define how the customer will perceive your products. The first impression is important. A good impression will mean more enquiries. You then need to improve on the conversion ratio. So, the first step is to prepare for the first online interaction or in-person meeting with the customer. I have often noticed people saying that the case is in the 'suspect stage'; hence, no preparation is needed to handle this opportunity. Your first impression is important. People go for a customer meeting without any preparation. To emphasise the importance of preparation, let us understand this from a different perspective.

The first meeting: It should be taken as seriously as a boy or girl will take their first date. There are certainly similarities between both of them. Both situations involve getting to know someone new and establishing a connection. In both cases, the goal is to leave a positive impression and build the foundation for a successful relationship.

First impressions matter: Just like on a first date, first impressions matter in a sales meeting. Dressing appropriately, being on time, and professionally presenting yourself can help establish credibility and build trust with the potential customer.

Establishing a connection: It is important to connect with the potential customer in a first sales meeting. This can involve finding common ground, asking questions without irritating the customer, and actively listening to their needs and concerns.

Building rapport: Building rapport in a sales meeting is essential. This can involve finding shared interests and engaging in friendly conversation to create a sense of trust and comfort. Do not try getting too personal and asking too many questions, which will make the customer uncomfortable. Control the temptation to say too many things without understanding the expectation first. Keep the meeting as relevant for the customer as possible.

Managing expectations: In both situations, it is important to manage expectations. In a sales meeting, it is important to be honest about what you can and can't do and to set realistic expectations for what the customer can expect from your product or service. Highlight the strengths and mention the shortcomings in brief, too. Sugar coat it so that they come to know about it without getting discouraged to proceed.

Follow-up: It is important to follow up after a sales meeting. This can involve sending a thank-you note or email, providing additional information or resources, or scheduling a follow-up meeting to continue the conversation.

By approaching a first sales meeting with a similar mindset to a first date, sales professionals can build stronger relationships with potential customers and increase their chances of closing a deal. The lead-to-conversion ratio can improve.

Stop Justifying Wrong Practices

To drive growth as an organisation, we must first accept our problem. When we pay no heed to our own organisation's inherent problems, we do not grow after reaching a size. The trend usually goes downward once the growth stops and the organisation plateaus. How do we escape this trap, which is so prevalent all across?

A regular business risk analysis is a must. Take people into confidence and talk to them about the potential business risks by outlining a few open-ended standard questions. Questions that will help you understand the competition, the strengths, the weaknesses, and the lapses. Compile that report and review that report once every year.

The leadership team remains ignorant of the seriousness of such issues until the revenue numbers grow. We pay attention to these issues when the business has started suffering the consequences of neglect. Many times, it is too late by then. One can only hope that the delay will not be so much that the organisation finds it difficult to come out of the negative growth momentum. Encourage your seniors to call a spade a spade and not sugar-coat it to such an extent that the meaning changes.

Importance of first-line managers

They play a vital role in the growth of your business. They are the eyes and ears of the organisation on the ground, and they need to stay driven and keep the frontline sales and support staff motivated enough to help resolve issues as much as possible within the given boundaries.

The role of the first-line manager should be clearly defined and empowered enough to keep the teams together. Suppose an organisation wishes to control attrition or introduce a new incentive scheme to push momentum during those seasons when sales traditionally get impacted. In that case, you need a strong first-line manager to ensure that this vision of the organisation gets implemented on the ground. He has to keep the team motivated, and the motivation has to work on an everyday basis. It is this motivation which will ensure the successful execution of any project.

Formal discussion on growth

Discussions on business growth are often neglected and rarely pursued. It is essential to discuss business growth regularly with relevant people who can contribute. Allow your field sales teams to share their challenges and suggestions with you using a bottoms-up approach. Compile them and discuss them without dismissing any issue as baseless. All suggestions should be taken as valid suggestions.

Write down the minutes of the discussion and discuss them if needed in subsequent meetings. Discussion on growth has to be an ongoing process and cannot be a yearly activity. When growth is not planned for, the company relies solely on the brilliance and abilities of individuals. When those individuals move out, the growth comes to a standstill. Quarterly or half-yearly business reviews are a good starting point for this and are being followed by many organisations.

Getting battle-ready

In the late 80s, there was a mushroom growth of PC manufacturers, who were primarily card-set assembly houses. They bought computer components and card sets from Taiwan, assembled them in small offices in India, and sold them to Indian consumers. The Indian IT industry witnessed massive growth in those years. Some of them had grown in size and stature.

The belief was that a salesperson should leave the office by 10 am and not return before 5 pm. The sales teams in many organisations left the office without knowing where to go and usually met in a common place near the office. Similarly, if they finished their work before time, most had a common joint where they would meet and wait. Once it was time, they moved towards the office individually.

Most organisations had no strategy to capture market share. Sales depended on the brilliance of a few individuals in the sales team. The result was that most of them had to shut down their business when they faced stiff competition. This was because they had never prepared to fight to win in a highly competitive market where the price was not the sole reason why people bought the product. They wanted quality, they wanted good service, and they wanted availability all across. These factors were cashed in by competitors like *Compaq, HP, IBM*, etc. even after selling at a 20-30% premium and thus, were replacing the Indian counterparts even in the home segment. The situation today is not very different in many organisations. No wonder thousands of organisations shut shop every year as they are not able to sell and earn money.

Spend money on sales and marketing to get a chance to meet and talk to more customers, or else the struggle will never end. Reward the team when they achieve their numbers and make them memorable if possible. Celebrate achievement in a way that more people in the organisation develop a desire to join them. Organisations have 100 percent club, where all those who achieve 100 percent of their sales targets in that year, get enrolled and are flown to a destination for few days of fun and frolic. You want the success stories to be remembered and repeated and not forgotten.

When we went to the Southeast Asian Countries, Latin America and North African markets to sell *Enterprise Software* for the banking and insurance companies, we were ready to invest in priming the market before making the first sale happen. We met the same customers multiple times, organised webinars and one-on-one sessions on technology's benefits, and explained how organisations across the globe benefit from such solutions.

This made us visible and helped us sign up with local partners and close deals.

Having said that, just because you are the first to introduce a product or service in the market does not give you much advantage, irrespective of what the management textbooks tell you. It needs to be supported by aggressive sales and marketing campaigns to grow in that market.

Poor financial management

While controlling expenses is crucial, it is equally important to exercise prudence and caution. These issues may seem basic, but their impact on the employees is profound.

For example, incentives should ideally serve as motivating factors. They become counterproductive when they become rare surprises that occur infrequently and lack transparency. Systems and processes should ensure that interference by individuals impacting the financial implications on select individuals is minimised if not eliminated. They affect the overall morale and motivation of the sales force. A transparent system fosters a positive work environment and promotes employee satisfaction.

In the heydays of PC assembling, *Escop Computers*, was one such organisation based out of M Block, Connaught Place. Rahul was an employee here who used to submit his local conveyance bills for clearance once a week. The finance person deducted 20% of the bill, and his logic was that Rahul overcharged by adding a few extra kilometers to his daily travel details. He cited how Rahul claimed 15km one day for going to the Okhla Industrial area, while he claimed 20km the next day for the same destination. So, he believed that Rahul had fudged the data.

In contrast, Rahul's justification was that there were multiple customers in the Okhla Industrial area, and sometimes, he had to return to the same place twice on the same day. This meant extra travel and extra kilometres in the claim sheet. The finance person was unsatisfied with this explanation and preferred reducing the claim. Grudgingly, Rahul agreed as he had no other option. The finance person was close to the organisation's owner; hence, too much of an argument could have other repercussions. This was a monthly ritual.

Even after over 30 years, meetings like these, where the salesperson is debating his expenses, incentives, etc. keep happening. The core problem remains the same. Misuse of finance should be checked, but hiding behind systems and processes to harass salespeople should also be controlled. Create transparency in all financial dealings. Organisations have more to gain than lose by doing so.

Lack of understanding and patience
Some invest in sales teams but may not know how to use them best and are sometimes in a hurry to get results. By brute force alone, they cannot achieve everything. So, shouting and yelling at sales teams to do their numbers is a sign of a less mature sales system, even though this method usually works in the short run. The negative impacts are hidden. Stop encouraging this habit among leaders and organise sales sessions to help them understand how to remain civil and drive revenue. The benefits can be seen in the long run in less attrition, increased business and a better work environment.

A baby needs nine months in the mother's womb. You can get the baby delivered in eight months, but nothing less, and you risk the baby's life. The same is true for business. So, plan accordingly. Give adequate time, effort, and resources to help it succeed. Have defined milestones to check the progress. Most importantly, put the right people on the job.

Overall, sales is an intricate process that requires a deep understanding of your target audience, industry, and business landscape. By customising your approach based on these factors, you can increase the likelihood of success and achieve better sales outcomes. Your leader should have an understanding of this. You have to trust your team and partners, and create a working environment where people do not have to spend much time thinking about internal unofficial issues. The defined systems should have the needed inbuilt safeguards. If they do not exist, then create them.

Do not encourage your teams to cheat their customers, partners, or colleagues. As a result, even simple tasks become complex, and teams spend too much time creating and sorting out confusion instead of focusing on business.

3

CHAPTER

The Seven Golden Rules

As per the *Udyam* Registration Portal of the Government of India, the total number of MSMEs that shut down between July 1, 2020, and July 18, 2023, stood at 24,839. The situation is similar in most countries around the globe. According to the Bureau of Labour Statistics, United States, approximately 20% of the small businesses fail within their first two years. The failure rate increases to 45% during the first five years and 65% by the tenth year.

Many businesses struggle with inadequate business planning and strategy. A lack of demonstrated differentiation in products or services can hinder their ability to stand out in a crowded marketplace. Similarly, without the right guidance and sales environment in the organisation, the sales team struggle to sell even if they have an excellent product.

One big issue is that customers do not come to know about the product's existence. Customers will buy only when they know that the product exists.

Furthermore, a limited understanding of expansion to new geographies or setting up partner networks and distributing products in different geographies stops them from growing their business.

In many cases, the difference between success and failure is a very thin line. Hence, understanding the success or failure stories help. Usually, failure stories do not get published and discussed, so we do not come to know about them and do not learn from them.

Learning from mistakes

Three friends started a company by the name, *Absoft India*. The aim was to do business in the area of Human Resource Development. It was decided that for the first few years one of the three persons will run the business until it reaches some point of stability.

The person from HR background was the first one to join. When he struggled for growth, he wanted the next person to join. Like many start-ups, he could not believe that success took time.

The next partner who replaced him was from a sales background. He found the placement job to be quite boring and found it difficult to provide any value addition or, for that matter, even focus on the business. He had got into the business thinking that the other partners would run the show and that he would only invest his part of the money, jumping in only when something interesting started happening.

The definition of interesting is always a challenge in such early stages. He tried doing some additional things to keep himself busy. So, he started software development and sales consultancy work, leaving the placement business to the team. He was now managing three lines of business — manpower placement, software development, and sales consultancy.

Soon, they were doing whatever came up as an opportunity, instead of focussing on a given area which they had chosen. They somehow managed and ran the business for a few years before giving up. Internal disputes on basic things became common in every monthly meeting. The business had to be shut down. Many do not shut down and keep dragging, although they never grow beyond a point.

This is a true story. This instance shows that what businesses need is a small checklist of basic things which many may know but most rarely follow. This list comprises the seven golden rules of success that should help any business to succeed. They have been outlined below.

1. Vision for growth

A clear vision for growth is the first and the most essential part of any journey. An idea alone is insufficient; it needs to be accompanied by a strategy that can be executed on the ground and supported by effective leadership to ensure that their focus does not waver when seeing difficulties.

Many believe that vision and mission statements are more of a formality needed during a company's formation. So, they write it and forget about it. In some cases, the Chartered Accountant doing the legal paperwork for the formation of the company writes it for them. However, if you want to grow, work on your organisation's vision and help your team understand what it is and how the organisation can achieve it. Let us understand why defining and discussing the vision for the organisation is so important.

Direction and Focus: A well-defined vision provides the entire organisation with purpose and direction. It helps align everyone's efforts towards a common goal and clarifies what needs improvement.

Strategic Planning: A vision serves as a basis for strategic planning. It helps identify key objectives and allocate resources effectively. It can help develop a roadmap with timelines to guide your business's future which people working with you will believe in. It can drive the exploration of new markets, products, and technologies, contributing to growth.

2. Managing finance

Managing finance in business with an iron grip, especially in the initial phase, is essential for survival. Poor cash flow management is the reason for many small business failures.

Despite effective financial management, small businesses often face cash flow challenges because everything seems essential, and it becomes difficult to differentiate between what is essential now and what can wait. For instance, a small manufacturing company that experiences increasing demand for its products must invest in additional machinery and equipment to meet this demand and expand its customer base. This upfront investment improves production efficiency, enhances product quality, and allows the business to fulfil larger orders.

Moreover, the company might need more staff to handle increased production and customer service requirements. While this is necessary for growth, it incurs additional expenses such as salaries, benefits, and training costs. These infrastructure and human resources investments are crucial for the business's long-term success but can strain cash flow in the short term.

Therefore, it is essential to understand that cash flow problems in small businesses can arise from poor financial management as well as from strategic investments necessary for growth. So, the need to borrow beyond your capacity arises. This is a tricky problem which businesses face and do not know how to handle. What is the alternate option they have?

An alternate recommended approach is to bite what one can chew. This means that one must be prudent in deciding how much risk one should take and how big the project one can manage without undue stress on the organisation's resources.

When you politely say 'no' to a big order, help the customer understand that how you want to commit only to what you can honour. The customer might feel good about it and either may support you financially by accepting the organisation's request for advance payment or might even place a more significant order later when your organisation is ready to execute larger deals.

Start-ups are known for their ambitious goals and innovative ideas, often requiring substantial financial resources to bring them to fruition. While this influx of capital can provide a vital lifeline for start-ups, it also comes with responsibilities and potential risks.

The next point is how to manage cash flow. Your target settings can be on an optimistic plan, but spending should ideally always be based on a realistic goal if not a pessimistic scenario. This will ensure you do not go out of cash very fast, as not everyone will be fortunate enough to have an endless supply of money.

There was a successful IT distributor in Rajasthan named *Unicorp* in the 1990s, a distributor for a globally renowned PC manufacturer named

Compaq. *Unicorp* was growing fast and wanted to grow even quicker, so it sold on credit while paying 100% advance to *Compaq*. Their growth became an example; from the outside, everything looked like a dream run.

Unfortunately, their customers started delaying payments, which impacted their cash flow. With reduced financial flexibility, they started defaulting on payments to their vendors. Slowly, they started losing grip on the market and, finally, had to shut down their business.

Managing finance is critical for the existence of your business. Minimise debt and outstanding payments at the same time. Investing in assets that can be used to liquidate and sail through bad times is also recommended. Every organisation goes through multiple rounds of bad patches; your preparedness for the rainy days will decide if you will continue to exist or become history.

3. Invest in sales and marketing

In establishing a business, there is a common tendency to assume that sales will naturally occur. The founders often lack a sales background.

The prevailing assumption is that the sales team will achieve results by any means necessary, as that is how the business needs to start. Consequently, these organisations fail to achieve significant growth despite initial excitement and struggle to meet sales targets. They often experience slow growth, contingent on having the necessary patience and courage, and may eventually collapse and close down.

Unfortunately, all the innovation and hard work put into these ventures go to waste. This raises questions about why many small organisations fail to scale up successfully and why some mid-sized companies stumble and collapse when they attempt to grow bigger. What is the underlying assumption in the sales process that goes so wrong?

There are three crucial things to consider here. A sales team should have three basic things in place. They are important for the success of your sales team.

Addressable Market: What is the size of the market you are trying to work on, and in which geography are they located?

Identify your target market to create a marketing strategy that enables you to reach them effectively. Making noise and gaining visibility in the addressable marketplace is possible only when you have a finite addressable market that can be mathematically defined. This will allow you to focus.

Avoid getting distracted irrespective of the temptation. Remember your sales team will have multiple reasons to stray and the most common reason is that they see opportunity in working outside the focused set of customers because of some reason or other. This will force your team to go thin, they will lose focus and will lose hold on the market, meaning poor sales and poor growth. The easiest method to control the temptation is by not financially rewarding the team for doing business outside the defined addressable market. One should be ready to lose some unplanned business in that process. Alternatively put a one person team to manage things which falls outside the definition, but do not allow your regular team to stray. A disciplined battle force always wins.

What is the compelling reason to act: A business must have something people want to buy because they need it and find value in the offering.

Try to solve one big problem of the customer. It can be a weight management pill that billions want or it can be a solution to save people from a common disease, or it can be as simple as an accounting software with analytics to help understand and manage business easier and better. It can be anything which is a big problem for the addressable market where customers will agree to spend money to buy the solution. Find the gap in the market and offer the solution.

Marketing to create visibility: The marketing team should work towards creating visibility for the product.

Participation in industry meets or leveraging the chamber of commerce and participating in their internal functions or monthly meetings by sponsoring lunch or dinner is an economical way of gaining visibility.

Even an unconventional mailer exercise can also work. For example, one of the organisations wanted to address identified 100 CEOs through their mailer campaign. They bought a small gift, a wooden boat, inside a glass bottle. They added a small note explaining the gift and explaining the product they wanted to sell.

Sent as a courier, nicely packed with the name of the CEO mentioned on it, most of them reached the designated tables. Those of whom were travelling, their secretaries took a special interest in ensuring its safe upkeep. It created the needed impact. The gifts cost more than a standard mailer but were an effective way of reaching out to the intended audience. The gift was such that it also impressed the family at home. So, every time the CEO looked at the gift, it reminded them of the company that had sent it. That's the power of effective marketing. It gets you space in the mind of the decision-maker. Selling becomes easy.

If people after trying your product do not decide to buy it in more than one occasion, you need to get worried and relook at the product, its positioning, and its usefulness for the market segment. You may even like to revisit your sales strategy. Getting rid of people should be the last option.

Keeping the sales team motivated is one big challenge. When business is not happening, they struggle more. The biggest payroll expense should be on the sales team for every new organisation in the first few years. You need to sell first to survive.

4. Training of internal and external stakeholders

Your team, partners, and happy customers are essential for the success of your business. Training programs will help them in doing their job better. Many organisations do not succeed as they do not know how to articulate their offering to customers properly. It is a common mistake for organizations to assume that their employees already possess the knowledge about a new product or solution, and hence do not require any special training. It is important to note that if customers do not understand the value of the product or solution in comparison to its competition, they are less likely to buy it.

Your customer-facing team should have a story to tell your potential customers and partners. It needs to be prepared, practised, and only then delivered. Similarly, run awareness sessions for your internal stakeholders like employees involved in developing or delivering the product or solution to ensure everyone is aligned with the company's goals and messaging. Here are a few reasons why training is important.

a. Consistent messaging: Training ensures the messaging to the customers and others is consistent. This consistency builds trust and credibility.

b. Product knowledge: Training helps internal stakeholders understand the product or service, its features, and its unique selling points. This knowledge equips them to effectively address customer queries, overcome objections, and highlight the product or service's value.

c. Confidence and motivation: Employees trained on the value proposition feel more confident in their abilities to represent the company and its offerings. This confidence translates into better customer interactions, increased motivation, and higher chances of success in selling the product or service.

Create a training portal and upload all needed information to help all stakeholders do self-training. Support this form of training through online or classroom training to improve effectiveness.

5. Ownership as authority and accountability

Build a culture of taking ownership of the respective work assigned to people. Have a clear definition of authority and accountability in the organisation to ensure that when your business starts growing, you have people whom you can trust and delegate responsibilities to.

Imagine a shopkeeper who wants to open two more shops. He cannot be physically present in all three shops simultaneously. He needs people who will do that. People whom he can trust. The same is true for any business. So, start working on it from day one and give merit a chance so you do not have to regret the extended arms failure to deliver.

Missing effective delegation can have consequences. Somewhere, there is a lack of trust, hence the desire to control every activity. This does work until a given size. However, it also creates smart executives who will never own up and take full accountability.

Smart executives keep their bosses in the loop for every decision-making, and they do it so that the senior person starts taking ownership of the transaction and the decision. This ensures that if the decision is proved wrong, the smart executive can quietly wriggle out of the situation, and the senior person will be busy defending both the executive and the conclusion. The problem with this approach is that your 'smart executive' neither learns the art of decision-making nor garners enough courage to face failure.

So, the next time when something like this happens, the senior person should help but ensure that the smart executive is held responsible for the success or failure of the decision. This will make that person accountable for their choices and slowly will be able to act independently, too. However, when you do not let the executive learn how to handle a task, the person can become a liability. Instead of reducing your workload, the person might add to your mental pressure when you want to outsource the leadership role.

Make your teams accountable for the work they do. It will help them and help the organisation.

6. Trust your team

Fostering a culture of trust, fairness, and open communication is crucial for maintaining a healthy and productive team environment. Encouraging collaboration and ensuring everyone has an equal opportunity to express their views promotes transparency and respect among team members.

In 2002, *ELX Linux*, a Hyderabad-based Linux start-up, hired a Sales Head from the industry to drive business. They had a Linux desktop that *Desktoplinux.com* rated as the best in the world. Everyone reported to the Founder, and no defined systems and processes existed. The Sales Head started with the sales rigour of visiting customers, talking to new potential partners, and all the things needed to help start selling a product. The sales began improving, and this is when everyone who had some say in the organisation's internal affairs, officially or unofficially, jumped in to provide advice and guidance.

The interference was bothering the Sales Head. In one such discussion, he lost his temper and his job. The Venture Capitalist, the CEO, and his advisors thought that they now understood how to grow the business and would be able to manage the situation well. Ultimately, after less than two years, the organisation had to be shut down. This was a sad end to a potentially promising organisation.

The lesson here is – don't go by hearsay. If you disagree or hear something negative about the leader, call for a formal meeting and discuss the issue before you decide to take sides. The desire to be the jury, judge, and executioner in any given issue can be bad for business. Talk to all parties concerned before you make a judgment call. Remember that going by hearsay is a huge problem in most organisations, big or small, so take it very seriously. Do not allow this culture to prevail.

A *Gallup* study found that organisations with high employee engagement and trust levels are 21% more productive. When individuals feel safe to take risks and share unconventional thoughts without fear of judgment or retribution, it promotes creativity and encourages meaningful out-of-the-box thinking.

7. Invest in quality

Selling quality products and solutions that work per the organisation's defined standards is the first logical step towards winning more customers and getting more business. Your quality standards should be so high that if the product fails, your team should not hesitate to replace it. They should know failure of the product or service is an exception and not the rule.

In 1999, my wife and I walked into a shopping mall in Princeton, New Jersey. We bought a mixer juicer under an ongoing offer, which was the last day. We were happy with the price performance offer and came home with it. When we tried to use it the next day, we found that the piece was faulty. On the subsequent day, we returned to the store and showed them the defective piece.

The salesperson apologised and gave us an option of either taking a refund of the money or picking any mixer grinder now available at a higher price without paying anything extra. We were highly impressed by this ethical behaviour of the store.

This ensures you get repeat sales orders and helps in spreading the good word, which is more impactful than any advertisement.

Selling quality products creates an impression in the minds of the customers that is difficult to erode by any competition. This helps cement an organisation's presence in the market and any competition irrespective of size and financial muscle will struggle to break that bond between the seller and the buyer.

When customers do not trust the quality, they do not recommend it to others. This is why even after many years of existence; some businesses struggle to add the next new customer.

Many years back in Hyderabad, I went for a sales training session, where they explained the meaning of 'customer'. The customer, they said, was equal to *kasht* (trouble/harassment in Hindi) + *mar* (death in Hindi). The implication was that someone who dies of trouble and harassment by the sales organisation is known as a customer! We all laughed and nodded our heads. In a room of around 60 experienced sales professionals, no one objected to it. We all agreed that the statement resonates with real life, and if we can do better and work toward customer care, things will improve for everyone.

Fix the pending issues when you have time. When business starts faltering, it may be too late to react. So, think like an ant and plan for the rainy day before the rain starts. Not everyone can survive rainy days without preparation.

Conclusion

Overall, one needs to be clear that by sitting in the same room where sales people sit, you do not learn sales, just as by staying in the same housing society where doctors live, you do not become a doctor. Hire a sales team to manage the sales. Train them before they hit the market.

The biggest challenge with the founders of products is that they fall in love with their creation and refuse to look at the issues and concerns which can drag them down. They become like the mother of the child whom nobody likes and still the mother can't see any fault with the kid. However, this can also be the reason why founders do not give up on their dream projects and succeed. There are no easy answers, but knowing the potential problem area can help.

4
CHAPTER

From Oblivion to Nirvana

The science of sales is so vast and different depending on the geography, product, people, and so many other things that one can feel completely lost. Many organisations get into selling without knowing how to make the sales happen. They do not plan for the challenges that they can face when they go out to sell. Hence, many brilliant products and solutions never succeed. In some cases, the product and solution were not so good to begin with, and hence, the market rejected them.

Vasundhara Enclave, New Delhi, is a residential area with a mixed population of middle-class and upper-middle-class families. There are around 44 housing societies, six markets, nine to ten schools, two government colleges, and one hospital. There wasn't any good multicuisine restaurant where people could sit and eat.

One restaurant appeared in a prominent location in one of the markets, where they started serving North and South Indian cuisine. The owners assumed they would get flooded by customers when they announced their presence. They expected 2% of the residents to visit their restaurant every month. Which meant around 1000 customers a month. However, that did not happen. When the restaurant did not see the needed rush in the next few months, they decided to shut down the business.

This has happened on more than one occasion. The same thing happens with many businesses. The owners should know that the success of a restaurant, like any other business, depends on multiple things. Making good food is just one of them. One has to create awareness so that people know the restaurant exists. When customers come to the restaurant, the way they are greeted, the way the food is served, the time you take to serve, and the quality of assistance provided if the customers ask for it are some other factors. The freedom of the team to waive off a given charge or the option to give a dish for free to a few select customers once in a while can help make it a memorable visit. Follow-up messages informing the customer about special occasions and special offers, etc., all play a part in making a restaurant successful, not just the food. The same is true for any business. There are multiple factors which will decide the future of your business. People get bogged down by the different issues and concerns and miss the forest while looking for the tree. No one thing can ensure success.

Feeling overwhelmed when faced with a vast field like sales is understandable. So, plan your approach. Break it down into small steps which can be executed and monitored.

Crafting your sales approach

In your sales pitch should you first present the organisation, the promoters, the kind of people you have, including your presence in India or globally, etc. and then go and explain the products and solutions, or start with the problems you can solve for the customer?

Define the time you think the customer will spend with you or your message and divide the communication time and content so that the potential customer can go through that message. You can then be sure of holding the attention span of the individuals without them getting bored and switching off within that time.

If you spend too much time discussing the corporate profile, the customers might get bored and not focus on what you can do. Alternatively, they may not know who you are if you focus only on the business problem. Customers can doubt your credentials and may not believe what you are presenting, more so, if it is too good to be true.

If you are not a well-known organisation, try focusing more on the business problem you can solve and less on the corporate profile, as your global competition may have a better profile than yours. They may have a bigger team, more existing customers, and more verticals where they have a presence. You may get outclassed very fast. So, work on the solution and focus more on that.

This is true even for selling a new TV or refrigerator in the showroom. An unknown brand offering good features may struggle to sell if the customers find it difficult to trust the organisation that made the product. So avoid exaggerating the benefits. It can be counterproductive.

In 1987, when I joined the IT industry, there was one prominent feature of *Intel* motherboards we emphasised while selling PCs – the processor's speed. It remained so for many years. Customers assumed everything else would be the same, so discussing other aspects was much less in most sales. With time, things changed, and people needed to highlight more than just the processor's speed. The matured customers and markets expect more. The learning is that what worked in the past may not always work in the future, so you have to keep your eyes and ears open and change your approach accordingly.

The sales pitch

This is the art of keeping your meetings engaging and productive. In a fast-moving world, your opening sales pitch should help customers understand what they are getting into. Once you have got their attention, support it with the value proposition and other things. Getting the customer's attention in an overcommunicated world is important for your product. Please keep it simple and crisp. Stating product functionalities cannot be the pitch. It must help understand why the customer should buy the product and how it will help. A short pitch is not necessarily good if it does not create curiosity to explore the product.

Emphasise details on high-value products. If the cost of the product is such that one needs to plan to buy it, ensure you are providing enough feature benefit lists to help the customer decide in your favour. When customers with enough financial resources are unsure about the product's value or the solution, the decision-making starts getting delayed. The low-cost, fast-moving products should have a small document explaining and re-emphasising the need and value of the product. The customer needs reassurance that they are making the right decision. The brief document should help, and so should your customer-facing team's positive attitude.

The pitch should be customised based on the demography. What works in North America may not work in many geographies outside the West. For example, in North America, manpower is very expensive. Any solution that helps in saving time, leading to reduced manhours to get work done, will get priority, but the same may not always work in many other countries, including India. If needed, the team can be asked to put in extra hours to complete a given work, and most will be forced to oblige without any cost implication on the business. So, think hard about what you should pitch and how.

The next important thing in pitching is the duration of the pitch. One needs to practice when to stop. One should refrain from saying everything the person knows, as that may become counterproductive. Similarly, one should know how much to write in a document.

Take the example of a guest who comes to your house. You offer the guest a cup of tea. To do that, you start pouring hot tea into the cup. The tea pot can hold multiple cups, but you only pour part of the teapot onto the cup. You are expected to stop once the cup fills. What happens if you do not control it? It will spill all over, and the hot tea might even hurt the guest and become a very irritating experience.

Similarly, too much of an explanation can be boring, and the potential customer may miss out on the main features. Unfortunately, the common practice many salespeople follow is that they don't stop sharing their knowledge without understanding whether the customer can understand, comprehend, and make sense of the pitch.

The pitch must also be based on the type of customer you are addressing. A knowledgeable customer needs to be handled differently compared to a novice. It might sound too elementary, but it is a common mistake made by the salespeople. They use the same pitch for every type of customer.

A long-extended meeting with your customer does not mean a successful meeting. You may not get the next meeting after that as the customer may want to avoid you after the long, boring meeting. Try to complete the meeting in the defined timeline and keep checking by asking questions if you are addressing the customer's problem.

Understand the sales process
Here comes the question of whom to sell, when is the right time to sell, what should be the route to sell, and at what price. Route here means whether the sale will be a direct one to the end customer, or will happen through the internet or follow the brick-and-mortar style, and if through a partner network, then what kind of partner network do you need to succeed? Thus, you cannot blindly copy any strategy. Check its applicability in your business and your geography. The issues are usually fundamental and very simple in many cases. We like to make it complex as organisations refuse to accept that they can be struggling with basic things.

The time needed to make a high-value or not-so-high-value sale can be the same or different, but the approach must differ. This needs planning and practice. We shall discuss that in the book later.

Different journey aspects
What kind of activities should the organisation focus on? When to focus on lead generation and when on lead progression? When and how to evaluate if the customer is moving towards a sale? What part of the work should be left to the backend team, and what part of the sales process should be driven by the sales leader?

Many such things are basic but important. Salespeople do not appreciate filling reports, so they may fill reports that are incomplete or, often, not very relevant. Making rules stricter is not the answer here. Finding ways to make them fill the least and making progress is what one has to work out if the salespeople have to work on a long list of potential customers. However, for big value enterprise cases, you may have different rules, and you should insist on filling in all possible facts which can help define the strategy for that opportunity. The assumption is that each salesperson will not have many high value opportunities to work on.

The next big thing can be the geography one should go after and why. What should be the method to approach the market? The clarity in these simple things can help speed up the organisation's reach and growth or can become the reason for slow progress. If you do not have these rules defined already, start working on them. Use your past data and experience to create the guidelines.

Does that mean that following a process will guarantee success? It just means that well-defined processes help you manage the sales process better; nothing can ensure success. There are too many intangibles at play, and one cannot possibly predict the outcome.

Unlike math or chemistry, where a given formula will always have the same answer, the result can be different in two similar situations in sales. Hence, planning, strategizing, and engaging is necessary to minimise the chances of losing. They can never be eliminated.

How engaging is your storytelling?
Selling is also an art of storytelling. It would help if you had a story people would like to listen to. A story that will convey what you are trying to sell and why. A good story based on lies can only succeed for a short time. Hence, avoid getting into such traps and doing anything requiring much reliance on lies. This can be a sure-shot recipe for disaster. So, your story should be based on truth. You can do minor twists, but you are not allowed to tell lies.

Your storytelling should touch the heart of the customer. Spend time and effort in building that storyline about your product or solution. One follows a similar strategy even in elections. Most people strangely do not go by data and facts; they listen to their heart. Hence, logical discussions seldom change the political supporter's mind. The heart rules the mind in most cases. Perceptions become more important than reality.

People vote for those they like; they usually do not vote for good governance, even though a poor leader can mean hardship for the masses. Hence, things change slowly in most parts of the world. This happens every day around the world. Similarly, a product with the maximum features, the best user interface, or the lowest price is not always necessary to win the battle. To make sales happen, communicate your story in a way that gets appreciated. Customers should fall in love with your product or service, or organisation. So, win your potential customer's heart through interesting stories about your product or service or customer relation or anything else which they would like to discuss and feel good about.

Connotation and denotation

Business organisations use multiple methods of communicating a message to their audience, including their employees, customers, and vendors, and often do not get the desired result. One needs to continuously check if what you are communicating and what others are getting is the same. If there is a difference between connotation and denotation, you have a problem that needs to be fixed on priority.

In the early 90s, a top-rated IT company named *Softek* created an advertisement campaign about SIMS – complete form being *Softek's* Integrated Management System. It had modules like accounting, inventory control, payroll, material requirement, and planning. The product suite was reasonably popular and was an excellent solution for business houses.

They hired *Ogilvy Direct* to come out with a campaign. An advertisement for SIMS appeared in the print media with a picture of a football game in action, featuring some of the leading global football players. The advertisement wanted to convey how the world-beating football teams work to win matches, in the same way SIMS would work for the organisations who buy them.

Many customers could not understand this. They used to ask the salespeople if *Softek* was in some way involved in the football World Cup and if they could help get them a free pass for the game. The story's moral is that you do not guarantee success by hiring one of the best advertisement agencies and talking about some of the best players in the world. It can turn out to be confusing for many.

Similarly, in early 2000, when *IBM* released an advertisement campaign on TV to promote their solutions in Linux, they talked about technology benefits that many could not understand. They found the advertisements to be very confusing. The advertisements may have been too advanced for the time.

Hence, the question is what you want to communicate and how? Will the intended audience have any interest in listening to the communication? If your product is good and you can effectively communicate it to the intended audience, selling will become easy.

Managing customers

Selling involves solving a customer problem which, many times, the customer does not know how to articulate and tell you and, many times, does not intend to share with you. Coming up with a wrong solution will make you lose the potential business. One should know that there are different dynamics at work around us; hence, what you see may not be what is happening. Talking to more people in the customer organisation is one important step to help clarify things for enterprise customers. For small-value or online sales, an aggregate of multiple customer feedback is preferable to talking to one expert to reach any conclusion. Help your potential customers understand the problems which you are solving. An online helpdesk to answer queries can be even better. Avoid putting an untrained BOT please, which has become quite common now a days.

Some of us wonder why the Enterprise customer will not correctly tell the seller the business problem. There can be multiple reasons for that, and one reason could be that the person concerned does not want the project to succeed. The second reason could be that they do not wish to have a specific vendor succeed, and finally, not everyone is good at articulating the problem correctly. Human beings are complex creations and behave differently under different circumstances, and many times, even in the same circumstances, they can behave differently to different people.

Similarly, one can send a team that cannot understand what the customer is trying to tell you and what they expect from you. Out of multiple issues raised and discussed, the solution delivery team may fail to understand the problem.

So, you need people who will ask the right questions and have the necessary skills to solve the customer's problem. Sending unskilled people to solve problems can lead to more problems.

In many online sales portals in this country, final billing becomes more complicated than selecting the product. Big giants like *Amazon* and *Flipkart* have developed the right software to help people. However, many small vendors have made things so complex and cumbersome that without help, a customer may find it difficult to buy anything. Such basic but critical aspects are overlooked for a long time, impacting business. So it is not always that complex problems not visible to leadership only create customer relationship problems; often, even such basic things are overlooked, impacting customer relationships and business.

The importance of follow-up

The reason for winning or losing a sale can be many. The objective should be to minimise the chances of losing a deal, especially if you have a perfect fitment of solution and price. One important aspect is following up with the customer without irritating them. Follow-up does not mean you send someone to bother the customer or call up without knowing what was discussed earlier. Do your homework and stay in touch with your customer.

Once, *Labsoft India* wanted to buy a software solution and invited a few organisations to discuss and understand their possible options. After due diligence, they shortlisted two organisations they thought had the needed skills and understanding to execute the project they wanted. So, the Chief Information Officer of *Labsoft India* invited both organisations – *Unicomp* and *PCL* to discuss his concerns. They had a two-hour meeting with both. After the meeting, there was complete silence for the next two months.

The leadership at *Unicomp* asked the salesperson to visit *Labsoft India* and find out if they could do anything. When the representative visited *Labsoft*, he was surprised that they had already bought the solution from *PCL* just a week back. The leadership of *Unicomp* rushed to meet the CIO and to find out why they were not given a fair chance.

Unicomp Sales Leader: We had the assumption that we had understood the problem and gave you a tentative idea of the solution you liked, hence, you will consider us for business. However, we did not hear from you.

CIO of *Labsoft*: I met two organisations, and one was yours. After the meeting, there was complete silence from your side as if you guys had reached a stage of nirvana, whereas *PCL* sent me a summary of the discussion along with the possible next steps. I found that impressive and started discussing it with them.

Unicomp Sales Leader: If you had told us you needed a summary, we could have also given you one.

CIO of *Labsoft*: I did not ask the *PCL* team to send me anything either. They took their interest and created that summary. Then, they followed it up to explain the outline with their suggestions. If they were so serious about our business, maybe they were the right people we should work with. Hence, I gave them the purchase order. I would have been happy to work with your organisation but was afraid that you would be more expensive, and then you never returned.

This is just one classic example of what, many a time, salespeople do. No notes are taken, no summary is created, and no options are explained to the customer.

In brief, they do not build the opportunity in a way where regular follow-ups are possible. In a low-cost product, you may automate the process; in a high-value product, you should put a person on the job to follow up. If you run a partner-led business, then check if your partner is making the same mistake and, hence, is not closing enough deals.

Preparing the business plan

Focus on your addressable market based on your strengths. People tend to pick the data points of the global leaders and put a percentage of their achievement as the possible market they would be chasing and closing. One should not use the achievement of the global leader as your benchmark to determine your share of the pie. Remember that you are not the global leader; hence, any comparison with them is only misleading. Just because you think your product or service is as good as the leader's offer does not make you eligible for the worldwide market pie. Prepare your organisation for the standard boring journey of identifying the Universe of customers, lead generation to lead progression to managing competition and winning deals. This is the most difficult journey. Try to make it exciting and interesting in real life and speed up the customer acquisition process.

Achieving nirvana is difficult

Sales is not a one-way street. A long-term business model requires giving a part of your earnings back to society. The goodwill that comes with it can prove beneficial in business, too.

Reaching a billion-dollar revenue in turnover is a long journey that involves pain, love, freedom, struggle, and everything else. The roller coaster ride with 360 degrees flipping occasionally is a norm. It tests your physical fitness as well as your mental toughness. Success takes you closer to the stage of nirvana.

The plan to add a new line of products or enter a new market segment may not work out. You may need to reinvent yourself, revisit your journey, and fix issues that are not letting you succeed. So, document the sales journey and revisit it. Rotate a part of the team, including the leadership.

Most organisations do not read the writing on the wall, do not change their approach. This is one primary reason for poor growth, unhappy employees, and unhappy customers. So, how does one reach the stage of nirvana?

Nirvana is a term that refers to a state of enlightenment or liberation from suffering. Despite being a profoundly spiritual concept, general principles can be applied to people's development and organisational growth. Listen to your people, partners, and customers, and incorporate changes per suggestions that may help you create a more positive and supportive environment, which is also needed for hyper-growth.

Of course, reaching the state of nirvana is a lifelong journey, and there is no one-size-fits-all approach to organisational growth and improvement. Being honest with your work, employees, customers, and business partners helps move in that direction. Learning from others' successes and failures is equally vital in this ever-changing, dynamic business world. It helps broaden your horizons and can help you grow your business. So listen, learn, think and apply.

5
CHAPTER

Trash the Management Books

Most management schools around the globe follow textbooks primarily written by authors in the West. The US plays a significant role in this, followed by some European authors. There are mainly two reasons for this. The US and a few Western European countries dominated global business in the last 100 years, and hence, they could easily impress upon the rest of the world to follow what they thought was right. Thus, the influence of western management was prevalent. They did not however, tell us how they also used military might to dominate the business world, which is slowly becoming increasingly complex now and cannot be used that easily for doing business with other countries.

The British East India Company traded in India not based on fair play but using military power. They entered to do business, took advantage of gullible Indians, manipulated the royals, and used their army to enter a different contract. A contract that was usually one-sided. They then used their media houses to start coming out with convincing storylines enforcing what they were doing in such a way that people started believing them to be better in every aspect of life. Whatever they said became gospel truth, and the world followed them without questioning them. The world was listening to one side of the story.

So, it was not an even playing field where they won against the competition. With the changing nature of competition, western countries are slowly losing grip on global business. Hence, the Western management style and their teachings on sales management are not helping them compete and win against the rising East. Why do you still see violence in many African countries over the raw materials and resources they have? Their gold, diamond, platinum, uranium, etc., are highly priced in the rest of the world, while the African countries possessing them hardly benefit from them. Do you know that out of the top ten diamond-producing countries in the world, eight are in Africa?

Who is taking them away, and how? Who is trying to control them? The world of commerce will be dominated by those who can control the supply of these essential raw materials. The business world is not just about buying and selling, as mentioned in the management books; too many variables are at play. However, we will primarily focus on the essentials of selling as there is a place for fair play, too.

The changing landscape of global business

We should have understood those books were written from a Western cultural perspective and under different circumstances. The authors did not write the books based on the local management issues and concerns of the rest of the world. Unlike machines, human beings behave differently in different geographies. So, how can they follow the same books to learn the secret of creating successful organisations in other parts of the world?

How will the developing economy grow business and manage competition with the limited resources they have at their disposal? Most of us do not have an answer, as we do not have enough books to refer to.

We must create our best practices and management books to make this transition, which will also work for us in our respective countries. We have to mix and match our education system and our orientation. We have to add our local components, our local issues and concerns, and our local way of managing them to drive globally successful corporations.

As of 2021, the population and land mass of the United States and selected Western European countries versus the rest of the world show that less than 10% of the population is dictating their management methodology to 90% of the world. This is one of the reasons why a significant portion of the world population outside these select few countries cannot become economically stable. They need to learn more ingenious ways to manage their workforce and resources in their given circumstances. When we do that successfully, we create history. Let's pick one example to understand this.

Adapting to local realities

In 2006, Baba Ramdev and Acharya Balakrishna started a pharmacy that sells Ayurvedic medicines named *Patanjali* in the small city of Haridwar. Neither of them had any experience running an FMCG company nor had any fancy degrees. So, their mind was not focused on the typical case studies and those so-called scientific management principles.

Their focus on quality Ayurvedic products at an affordable price, leveraging low-cost distribution centres and a relaxed work environment, became a game changer. Baba Ramdev became famous by offering free yoga classes through television and gaining the masses' trust. They used word of mouth and social media to increase visibility and became a 1.4 billion dollar, fastest-growing FMCG organisation in India by 2019-20. The learning from this story is that one does not need to read fat books on management written by Western authors to learn about running a business successfully.

His years of practice in Yoga and a tie-up with an equally dedicated person trained in Ayurveda created the magic. Baba Ramdev leveraged his skills for the good of the masses and used that goodwill to give some of the biggest names in the FMCG business in this country a run for their money. It also proved that Corporate Social Responsibility, if done with sincerity, does help the business.

Teaching Yoga by Baba Ramdev was a CSR initiative where he gave back to society without expecting profit. It worked, as people started trusting him and anything associated with him. They believed *Patanjali* would not cheat their customers so they could buy their products. This belief worked like a wonder drug, and the rest is history.

In another discussion with a doctor in a government organisation responsible for medical research, we found a fascinating story of why we should not blindly follow what works in a faraway land without really checking it out, which may not be very easy every time, but is necessary.

The Indian Council of Medical Research, a government healthcare organisation, wanted an Artificial Intelligence or AI-based software that could check the scanned image of a given body organ for tuberculosis and predict if the person needed immediate attention.

A company in South Africa was found, which claimed 90% accuracy for such cases. So, they decided to test it in India before buying the software. The result was only 25% accurate and not 90% as claimed. This happened because of the fundamental difference between people in South Africa and India. Due to its unsuitability for Indians, they decided not to proceed with this solution.

However, in the case of management books, we have yet to check their suitability for our country.

Limitations of Western Management and their books

These management books and case studies showcase one side of the story. Most of the time, they assume that the brightest and most brilliant will work with you. So, they reward the select few and punish the rest. Despite wealth and prosperity in Western countries, there are many unhappy and poor people because of this thought process. The underlying fear is such that, at times, it takes an ugly turn in the form of racism or depression and leads to unwanted violence like mass shootings. This belief that there is no place for mediocrity in business may not be accurate. Most giant organisations' survival largely depends on ordinary people who can be termed mediocre. The method of involving them and growing the business can be different. Hence, we also need books and methodologies to work with modest people.

Management books give you one perspective when any such case study or management topic can have more than one perspective. Western books and magazines have created a world that doesn't exist in most parts of the world, and when you run your business based on these guidelines, the result is usually poor.

Creating local best practices

Countries have different cultural values and ways of life; hence, one must learn and understand how things work in these different geographies based on their peculiarities. That is why many leaders who are helping build a huge multi-billion-dollar empire in the West are failing to do so in India or other smaller nations worldwide.

Learning and understanding the culture of a different country or different Indian state is vital for any business. First, it can help you avoid misunderstandings or unintentional offence when interacting with people from that culture. For example, what might be considered polite in one culture may be rude in another.

Even the fundamental behaviour of people in different states of India differs. People in the National Capital Region are more aggressive than those in the north-eastern part of India. People in the west are more business-oriented compared to people in the eastern states and many other states of the country. You need a different approach to doing business in different parts of the country. So, you need to learn the cultures of different states of India if you wish to do big business in India. The same is true for other parts of the world.

I have worked with countries across the globe. In some countries, we found that when we presented a software solution to potential customers, a solution they needed, only some asked many questions, and most remained silent. After investing much time, effort, and energy, we found that people prefer to avoid telling you that they are not okay with your product, pitch, or solution as they think it will be impolite. So, when they say nothing, it can mean that they have not understood anything or they have not liked your solution at all, irrespective of the fact that what you are offering is something that can help them solve a significant business problem at an economical price point.

Our experience in Australia was precisely the opposite. They first wanted to know if we had a local presence. Second, they wanted to know how we were better or how we compared to the global market leaders. They stopped us in between if they did not find the going to their liking. So, your preparation for every call was critical in a developed market compared to a developing economy. Even the dealer or partner community behaved differently. They were not interested in working with a new vendor without checking the direct market presence of the organisation they needed to represent. They want to see the effort which the organization is putting on their own to reach out to the customers. Ground presence which is visible was very important. Having team members who are of the same colour and ethnic background as the majority are also a great help. So in Australia hire Australians and in Saudi Arabia hire Arabs for customer facing roles. However, no management book tells you about all these challenges, which an organization from a developing country will face while trying to sell in the developed countries.

The story's moral is that we should understand that the same management principles do not work everywhere, as people, local cultures, and their way of life differ from what we learned in our management lessons.

Take the example of any fast-food joint like *McDonald's*, *Domino's*, or any other store. The standard questions the person on the counter across the United States will ask is 'for here or to go', meaning do you want to eat it in the restaurant or want to pack it and go. This is helpful; national standardisation helps the counter salesperson and the customer. However, this standardisation may not work in many other parts of the world.

If you try defining something similar in India, it may not work, as people do not like following unquestioningly. They will argue and debate about everything. So, implementing something fundamental like this can be a challenge. Culturally, we behave differently; hence, the same style of functioning does not work here. The same is true for management principals, too.

Understanding and appreciating cultural differences is essential for building relationships, fostering empathy, and creating a more inclusive and diverse sales strategy.

Rethinking management principles

Let us look at a few examples of how the real business world works compared to what is mentioned in the management books to help us understand why we should trash the management books.

Experience and exposure can change the perspective of the leaders. This is something that many of us struggle to understand; hence, many believe that youngsters will be able to do what an experienced person is doing. This does help in cost cutting but does not help in growing business.

Experience is simply invaluable, with very few exceptions. Nothing can replace the knowledge and expertise that comes from hands-on practice and learning. Trust the power of experience and let it guide you towards success. Unfortunately, the standard management books do not define this aspect of life and business. This is a recipe for disaster.

In many countries around the world, decision-makers, when making critical financial decisions that can impact their cash flow, would like to talk to people with grey hair and deep understanding. Only knowledge is not important; optics are equally important.

In one of the global IT giants in India, the software business leader thought of converting some of the technical leaders into sales leaders, as the discussion with the customers did turn technical on many occasions. Things moved fine until the business kept growing; once the company started going down due to a change in the headwind, everything went out of control.

The technical leaders converted to sales leaders had never handled a situation of falling sales before as they had never owned that responsibility. They did not know how to manage the downturn of business. They had a disastrous year, and the leader had to quit and go.

Why most global giants are from select Western countries

Many global giants have historically emerged from select Western countries due to various factors. While it's important to note that not all Western countries have enjoyed equal success, the standout feature of certain nations has been their commitment to fostering a business work culture grounded in meritocracy.

These nations have excelled in providing opportunities and recognition to individuals based on their abilities, irrespective of their backgrounds or affiliations. This emphasis on meritocracy has allowed talent to rise to the forefront, driving innovation and efficiency in business operations. This culture of rewarding excellence has contributed significantly to the global dominance of some Western countries in various industries. Most developing nations around the world have failed to follow this simple policy and businesses have paid a heavy price on account of it. Unfortunately, we still refuse to change. One reason is that no management book actually tells you about the advantages of meritocracy over other methods.

Let us take up a few fancy tag lines, which are much talked about in the management books, and see how it works for many other countries worldwide, including India. We need to understand the complex interpretations they have.

Give your employees more freedom

Every employee loves this statement, and every big corporation likes discussing this point. The actual meaning can be quite complex, and implementing something like this without getting into intricacies can be disastrous. Freedom here means allowing independence within defined parameters and following defined rules, ensuring that you run in your predetermined circle, sometimes overlapping similar circles but not beyond that.

In organisations with solid systems and processes, where rules and roles of people are well defined and followed, where the approach to measure performance and reward or penalise people based on performance as the primary criteria are well defined, this approach will work. This can show excellent results, which is one big reason why many successful global giants can grow and expand their businesses.

The assumption that people understand their responsibility and will do things without monitoring them may be only wishful thinking. Giving too much freedom is counterproductive and is not usually the case even in most successful global giants. Space should be given within defined boundaries.

Most organisations need such robust systems to measure performance and reward people or penalise them for cheating the system. Hence, the point mentioned above is valid for only 2% of organisations around the world, and there is still so much discussion around it. Thus, there are no simple and standard answers. Freedom can get your organisation into a bigger problem than anticipated.

In 2017, Mombasa partnered with an Indian product company to do business in Burundi, Africa. The partner wanted that for all disputes, the jurisdiction would be the London, UK court, not New Delhi, India. This is against the standard protocol that the product company followed. However, without the knowledge of the Business Head, the salesperson signed the agreement by making this small change. Eight months later, the Indian product company wanted to sign up with another partner as the current one, Mombasa, was ineffective.

The next day, there was a mail from the London office of Mombasa in the Business Heads email box. They had challenged the new partner signing up, as one of his employees had joined this new organisation. They threatened the Indian product company with a court case. Even though it was a frivolous case and would not have stood the scrutiny in a court of law, imagine the cost of fighting this case overseas. Even if the Indian product company had to send their legal person a few times and hire a local lawyer to file a response, the overall cost could have been nearly hundreds of thousands of USD for nothing. Imagine getting into such a legal hassle just because of some oversight.

This does not mean you should stop giving freedom to people; it just means that this suggestion comes with a rider. Such incidents do not happen much in select Western countries, as people get fired for this. Their lives are lived in straightjackets of thinking. They do not improvise on the fly daily. Hence, there needs to be a new set of books for those countries where systems and processes do not work by default.

Catch them doing something right

In management jargon, they call it motivation. Usually, it is a top-down approach. A sales manager is expected to motivate his subordinates. He does that by catching the juniors who have done something good and praising them for that. There are thousands of books that talk about the importance of motivation. No one tells you about the pitfalls of praise, especially if you are a small or mid-sized organisation.

The strange thing I have noticed in some parts of the world is that when you praise a junior salesperson or employee for doing something good, they reduce listening and following instructions. They start believing that the organisation is dependent on them. Hence, they can take the liberty once in a while, which slowly increases and leads to indiscipline and, sometimes, makes the same contributor more of a liability. This does not mean that you should not motivate people or you should not 'catch them doing something right'. Without a motivated team, you cannot fight and win the competition. You need a motivated sales team to fight and win.

Exercise caution to ensure that your motivated employee does not start demotivating you or your fellow employees. Management books do not discuss this issue. Most Indian companies are more humane in running their business. The concept of firing employees at the drop of a hat is not that prevalent. Hence, they have to start thinking differently.

Now let us discuss what is not in the management books but should be there. What is it that the West forgot?

Have you motivated your manager today?
One needs to ask, what actions are the junior sales staff taking to motivate their managers. It is not that only managers have to motivate the sales teams down the line; the responsibility also lies with the junior sales teams. So, teach your freshers and juniors to do things that will act as motivation for leadership.

In 2010, *IBM* introduced the concept of a 'Small Deals' team. India was one country identified for this project. In the first quarter of execution, there were expected to be many hiccups as the team would take time to settle down. Everyone started putting in the needed effort.

This did help motivate the team leader. As a result, there was no shouting or yelling. The motivated team performed so well that they overshot their first-quarter sales numbers. The leadership was slightly surprised to see that.

This was possible because the team also worked hard and motivated the leader. There is value in being a supportive follower too. The relationship between the leader and the team is mutual; they must work towards the common objective without force or coercion.

This can only happen if the team members also do their part in motivating their managers. Add a chapter on this and help people think differently. This can help change the mindset of the juniors. Once this starts happening, the work environment will become even more cordial and friendly. This should also help improve the organisation's overall performance.

How to be a good follower
Enough has been said about sales leaders and their leadership skills. Leadership role looks like the ultimate goal. A senior person can bring much value to the system even as an individual. The management books must include a chapter telling people that not everyone needs to become a

leader. Living a happy life can be a bigger priority for many, and being a good follower also can be an aspiration.

Individual contributors are critical. So, there is no need to feel dejected about not becoming a people manager or focus too much on building people managers. This one-track approach has forced people to think in one direction and has created many leaders who do not deserve to be leaders.

Maybe they never wanted to be a leader in the first place. Still, the social structure of the society and the organisation, as created by the western-influenced management books, had forced them to become leaders. There are many unhappy followers and a miserable leader as a result of this. The promotion of a brilliant individual contributor to the role of a people manager throws that person off track when his skills are more suited to the role of an individual contributor. One unfortunate soul makes unhappier souls. It is infectious.

If leadership is essential for organisation building, having good followers is equally important. Good followers are vital to the success of any leader. So, building effective followers needs to be on the agenda.

Good followers can help compensate for their leaders' shortcomings. They can provide feedback and support that can help the leader to improve, and they can also help to implement the leader's vision and strategy.

Leadership is a two-way street, and good leaders need good followers. By being a good follower, you can help create an environment where people can contribute to the success of your organisation.

No guidelines or books tell the masses how to be a good follower and how it helps. So, I have laid a brief framework for becoming a good follower.

Be committed: A good follower is dedicated to the organisation's vision, goals, and values. Show your dedication by attending meetings, completing tasks on time, and being a reliable team player.

Communicate effectively: Working collaboratively with your leader and team requires effective communication. Listen actively, ask questions, and express your ideas and concerns constructively.

Be proactive: Take initiative and seek opportunities to contribute to the team's goals. Explore ways to improve processes and suggest innovative ideas that align with the organisation's objectives.

Support your leader: Even if you disagree with your leader's decisions, support them publicly and provide constructive feedback privately. Remember, criticism should always be given respectfully and professionally.

Remain positive: A positive attitude is important for creating a productive work environment. Avoid negativity and focus on finding solutions to challenges and opportunities for growth. Control your temptation to criticise leaders for every small setback. It only helps in spreading negativity, which is bad for business.

Continuous learning: To keep learning is essential for personal and professional development. Seek out training and development opportunities that will help you improve your skills and add value to the team.

These traits can help you build strong relationships with your leader and team, improve your performance, and contribute to the success of your organisation.

Understanding hypocrisy and sycophancy

Understanding these aspects is one of the most important things for every budding leader, including those in sales. One must know that great leaders have mastered the art of bombing a country and simultaneously discussing human rights and civil liberties.

Telling the truth about the bad decisions of your leadership team in any meeting, private or official, is not appreciated in most organisations worldwide, irrespective of what the vision and mission of the organisation written in the document hanging on the wall tell you. The challenge is that the middle-class value system in this part of the world teaches you to be otherwise and following that can cut short your corporate life.

Those few minutes of straight talking with seniors can cost someone their job. It is important to practice and learn to agree with seniors regardless of whether they agree, without expecting juniors to do the same. This can help control this behaviour in the workplace. This can take away the undue advantage many not-so-competent people get by practising the art of hypocrisy and sycophancy. People based on merit can get a chance, which is what organisations need to grow in a competitive environment. Lack of sycophancy is one big reason why many competent people only sometimes rise in the career ladder.

Sycophancy, or the act of overly flattering or ingratiating oneself to a leader or authority figure, can create a culture of dishonesty and insincerity, where people are more concerned with pleasing those in power than pursuing the organisation's or community's best interests. However, this is how the world moves and, hence, should be taught at an early age.

All of us know at least one person in our organisation who does not deserve to be a manager, or for that matter, in some cases, does not even deserve to be your junior but is growing and doing well in the organisation compared to those who are really very hardworking and sincere yet going nowhere. Being idealistic does not help people grow, so good guys often lose out.

Hypocrisy, along with sycophancy, is a complex art to be mastered and does not come naturally to performers. This is an art that needs to be taught. We desperately need books on this to be an essential part of management education so that the good guys do not lose out and can stay in the organisation and help the organisation grow much faster and better.

I am not trying to encourage these habits and would strongly suggest eradicating any organisation with such people; however, that would need another 100 years or so, even if we start today.

Hypocrisy in leaders occurs when there is a discrepancy between their words and actions. It is a common problem that can lead to loss of respect and trust from their followers, but it is common and done in a way that the masses can only understand the impact once it is too late.

Hypocrisy in leaders can manifest in various ways; the management graduates or the young leaders in the organisations should know that this is common and bad for business. Hence, identify and try to remove it before the damage is done. Wishful thinking, one can say. Learn it to understand it.

Not following your sermon is the most common form of hypocrisy in leaders, which goes unnoticed. In some cases, the sycophancy among followers covers it up and never gets noticed. For example, leaders advocate for ethical behaviour but engage in unethical practices themselves. Once you know the art and science of managing such people, you will not feel frustrated and will better manage situations.

Leaders who are inconsistent in their behaviour or decision-making can run businesses successfully in a less competitive environment. So, not all bad leaders force a shutdown of the organisation. However, good people who do straight talking can help make everyone's life better and would be good for the organisation and society.

For example, a leader who advocates for work-life balance but regularly works long hours. In a way, the leader sends a message that working late hours and not bothering about work-life balance will be appreciated more. Naïve but sincere young employees may fall into the trap and can suffer, wondering where they went wrong. Since such practices are prevalent, cutting across industries, a handbook and classroom workshops should help anyone and everyone.

Lack of transparency

Extremely important but missing from management books. It is common to see leaders share information on a need-to-know basis, which is why you have so much grapevine information moving around in the organisation. Thus, systems and processes are not defined, or if they are defined, they are not followed. This impacts sales as the teams concerned do not cooperate or help grow the business.

Leaders worry that if they are completely transparent, their actions and decisions will be scrutinised and they may face negative consequences, such as public criticism, legal action, or loss of support. Hence, they believe that presenting a particular image or perception is essential for maintaining their power and influence, even if it means withholding information or being less than transparent about their actions.

It is important to note that transparency in leadership is critical for building trust and accountability, which are essential components of effective leadership. When different sales leaders do not share information, they make selling more difficult. This starts impacting when an organisation goes through a bad sales patch.

In simple words, we live in a complex world. What we see and believe may not always be true, as we tend to see what we believe we want to see. This is why we have blind followers of leaders, political or otherwise, even among the educated masses.

The journey to becoming a better manager and leader is ongoing. By embracing diverse perspectives and continuously learning, you can adapt your management style to thrive in an ever-evolving global business landscape.

We have followed the books and teachings of the West for too long. However, most countries outside the West have either not succeeded or those which have, like Japan or China, have achieved as they have followed their way of running their business. They have created their localised rules and guidelines based on the realities of their daily life. One has to understand their culture, exposure to the masses, and the strengths and weaknesses of the people and work accordingly.

6
CHAPTER

Sales is a Science and an Art

The science of sales involves a scientific approach where you must define systems and processes that people will follow based on predefined rules. People will be treated more like an employee number and put in the system based on a predefined structure. The sales strategist must develop a strategy based on data analysis and research. This includes conducting market research, analysing sales data, and tracking customer behaviour to create a data-driven sales strategy.

The art of sales requires an artistic approach to build relationships, use storytelling, create engaging conversations, and connect with customers personally. The art of sales involves communicating effectively, inspiring trust, and conveying authenticity and empathy to customers, which requires developing soft skills such as active listening, kindness, and emotional intelligence.

To be successful in sales, the organisation needs to have a balance of both the scientific and artistic aspects of the profession. A sales organisation that combines a data-driven approach with a personable and engaging manner is likely more effective in connecting with customers and closing sales.

Emotional quotient

Unhappy customers are bad for business, damaging the organisation's reputation and impacting future sales. Hence, building the organisation's image over a period where you show that you care for your customers is a must.

Organisations should seek a high Emotional quotient (EQ) among their senior leadership. The organisation's culture always depends on the top; it flows downwards. Hence, if the senior leadership can understand the internal and external customers, empathise with them, and help positively resolve problems, it will help build a team that will do the same. This, in return, will have a healthy work environment and better relationship with customers and should ideally lead to more business. However, this will only happen when you have a system to ensure this culture develops in the organisation or it will take a lot of time to develop organically.

A word of caution here. High EQ does not mean you agree to unreasonable asks of internal or external customers to make them happy. Asks that cannot be honoured should not be committed. Here, the combined approach of science and art can help develop a leadership team that is more responsive to the organisation's needs while also being mindful of the customer's expectations.

Active listening

Encourage your customer-facing teams to listen actively and with empathy to their partners and customers. This means paying attention to their concerns and needs, acknowledging their feelings, and responding compassionately. Our biggest challenge is with salespeople who are keener on giving a sermon in any discussion and looking for ways to prove the other person wrong.

Encourage your team to build strong relationships with their partners and customers based on trust and respect. One can achieve this through regular communication, providing feedback, and demonstrating genuine interest in solving their problems.

Teams should know how to manage conflicts constructively and respectfully, such as through active listening and compromise at times if needed.

Building relationships with customers

It was around 1990 when I was part of the sales team of *Softek*, selling compilers to *Uptron* for their powerful 680x0 processor-based *Mightyframe* machines. *Softek* had developed a C Basic compiler for this machine, and I visited the *Uptron* Lucknow office to hand over the software for evaluation. Mr AN Khare was the senior manager responsible for the software team at *Uptron*. They were an IT vendor of repute in those days. His team had checked the software and found bugs in it.

On my visit to their Lucknow office, Mr AN Khare lost his cool and gave me a piece of his mind. He was very upset and shouted and yelled at the top of his voice. I was at the receiving end. I went completely silent and listened to him standing in one corner. Everyone in the big hall could hear his thunderous voice ripping me apart. I peacefully heard him, returned to our Delhi office, and shared his concerns with the Technical Director. The next version was couriered to them.

On my next visit, I was supposed to meet him again. I was worried and was mentally preparing myself for the second session. However, a strange thing happened. Instead of shouting and yelling, he took me to the cafeteria, had a coffee with me, and complimented me for hearing him out last time. He was happy to get the new version. After that, problem or no problem, Mr Khare never shouted at me. Things changed for good.

Mastering this art of managing difficult situations can help organisations win more hearts, make the customer-facing job simpler, and can become a potential game-changer. This will also help when working on a more significant project that is time-consuming, error-prone, and dependent on people skills.

Managing difficult situations

Many deals are won or lost depending on how good one holds the nerves in a crisis. This becomes even more important when the crisis with your customer is getting discussed across the table, especially with slightly unreasonable customers, tough negotiators, or harsh taskmasters.

Selling is an art; hence, one has to hone these skills by continuously working on them and taking professional help if available. There are various aspects of sales, and developing the sales team's skills is an important factor apart from having a good product line and sales strategy.

In older days, sales managers taught this art to a certain extent to salespeople by sending them to do cold calling. Cold calling is the first step in the school of sales, preparing one for the journey ahead. Struggle, humiliation, failure, and the guts to rise repeatedly are prerequisites for a person to succeed in sales. One needs to get used to facing the unknown.

With cold calling, the fear of facing the unknown will be reduced to a manageable level, as will the ability to handle nonsense. They will learn not to take the easy way by promising the wrong product or solution. They will not get tempted to cheat customers; they will usually not lie. They will not easily get intimidated. A confident team will help the organisation at all times to come.

When I started my career in sales in 1987. I managed the territory of Okhla Industrial Area, Connaught Place, and Wazirpur Industrial Area of New Delhi. In a day, I covered around 25 organisations. We used to pick a block and start from the beginning. Walking into every office and trying to meet the IT head or the owner of the firm, or the Purchase Manager even. Initially, crossing the receptionist in many organisations took much work. Sometimes, the guard outside the entrance did not allow me or my colleagues to enter in some factories and offices.

With time and practice, one learns to manage the situation; one learns the art of going past the gatekeeper and meeting the people concerned. Cold calling teaches you not to be demotivated even after consecutive failures to enter a given market segment. Today, when we travel to international locations, we often meet intimidating people. We do face situations that are not very comfortable. However, years of handling complex cases in a sales scenario have taught us to handle the situation without fear. We may be anxious but not afraid to smile and take the lead in the conversation. That is what cold calling helps you to become. It prepares you for the journey.

They realise and learn how to make a sale happen only when they step out into the real world. Stepping out in the real world and facing customers, even for an inside salesperson, is almost mandatory. It prepares him for better results.

Only when the rubber hits the road do you know the meaning of friction and the heat it generates. Not all tyres can handle it, and many burst and hurt the passengers. Hence, you need to use tyres designed for the type of roads you want to drive on. Similarly, until a salesperson meets customers, they won't understand friction in the sales world. Cold calling helps in adapting to new challenges.

Building and Managing Mega Organisations

As businesses scale up, they must be managed differently. It is difficult for many unicorns to manage their businesses after reaching billion-dollar valuations. We can learn from other industries. In fact, a few trade tricks should be observed in the huge public sector organisations selling and growing in a hugely competitive market.

We have the largest insurance company in the world, *Life Insurance Corporation of India*, running successfully in this country, catering to more than 290 million policyholders, as per 2019 data, and catering to their requirements successfully in most cases. *LIC* has its corporate office in Mumbai with eight zonal offices, 113 divisional offices, 2,048 branches, 1,430 satellite offices, and 1,227 mini offices.

There are lakhs of agents reaching out to the masses, even in far-flung areas of the country, to provide a personal touch and personalised service to their customers. By any measure, this is huge, and it's been running for decades, helping the government and the nation. The biggest brand names globally could not throw them out of business, which many believed would happen. They are still the market leaders in this country. Managing huge organisations successfully is a great example of our abilities. We should understand how they are structured at the regional and central levels. It is this structure that holds the organisation together.

Coming out with new schemes or policies is one aspect, but ensuring that they reach the agents spread across the globe and are selling the policy the leadership wants is an art and a science. Every growing organisation operating out of multiple offices selling multiple products need to learn from them.

Managing mega projects

We have also proved that we are quick to build a team for a given huge assignment, behind comprehension of most, and dismantle the team once the work is done. We need to do the same in business when we want to execute a new mega project where we need people from all other parts of the organisation or we need to hire temporary staff from outside. You can explore the option of hiring freelancers or partner resources to execute the project if your customer is okay with it. Some customers will be worried for the quality, data security and trade secrets aspect, hence this method may not work for all customers. Organisations are adopting these models to execute projects as that helps them execute mega projects without adding more regular staff.

An excellent example is the *Kumbh Mela*, or how the Election Commission conducts elections in this country. With 900 million people eligible to vote, we run the world's most crucial and most complex election. Almost flawlessly. The election commission of India sends people to remote locations of the country to ensure that every citizen is given a chance to vote.

This involves travelling through dense forests at times and trekking in the hills on foot, if needed, to reach those remote locations and follow the same system and process followed elsewhere in the country to help the citizens cast their vote. Our government officials who work as clerks, teachers, etc., are temporarily assigned to the Election Commission to assist them.

Their work includes setting up polling stations in remote and far-flung areas, as well as educating locals about the importance of voting in a democracy and showing them the latest electoral technology, such as the voter-verified paper audit trail (VVPAT).

Just imagine how the Election Commission of India manages to do this in every general election held every five years. This is a classic case study of motivation, perseverance, and dedication. They remain ethical and unbiased towards any political party and give respect to people from every strata of society. Hence, the participation of poor people in elections is very high across the country. The perception of being fair to all helps. Our mega business organisations should learn these best practices from them.

This proves that within this country, we have examples from which we can learn how to scale the business and manage them successfully, even in demanding and unfavourable circumstances. The business community should learn how systems and processes defined thoughtfully can help execute the most complex and difficult elections with temporary staff with almost no complaints from opposing parties. The same strategy can work for businesses when they want to create new divisions or temporarily create divisions to execute specific projects.

Organisations are often forced by competition and circumstances to venture into areas that are unknown to them. Some do not tread that path out of fear and lose growth. Venturing into the unknown with caution is always helpful and necessary to grow the business. At times, it can be slightly fearful. Fear is good for business. One needs to learn the art of controlling it rather than eliminating it.

Controlled fear of failure is good, just like the paratrooper in the Indian Army who is dropped behind the enemy lines during a war situation and does not know what kind of reception he will get. This fear makes him practice harder and keeps him alert. Similarly, in business, this fear can help us prepare better for the worst, and maybe that is what will make us succeed. We start falling apart when we become assured of success, stop taking precautions, and stop respecting the basic ground rules of competition. Complacency sets in when you witness growth, quarter after quarter, against all odds. This is the time when you should invest more in sales and marketing.

The art and science of selling go hand in hand. In addition to learning skills from personal experience, science can be harnessed by creating procedures, guidelines, and rules to guide the team in adhering to the rules of engagement, which can be checked and corrected as needed.

To truly master the art and science of sales, remember that knowledge alone is not enough – action is the key to success.

1. **Invest in your and your team's development**: Continue honing your sales skills, both scientifically and artistically. Consider enrolling in sales training programs, workshops on emotional intelligence, or negotiation seminars to expand your expertise.

2. **Implement new strategies**: Apply the lessons learned in this chapter to your daily sales activities. Experiment with data-driven approaches, storytelling, and enhancing your soft skills in real customer interactions.

3. **Seek feedback**: Don't shy away from constructive criticism. Encourage your peers, mentors, or supervisors to provide feedback on your sales techniques and communication skills.

4. **Stay informed**: Stay up-to-date with the latest developments in the sales field, including emerging technologies, market trends, and customer behaviour shifts. Attend industry events to learn how competition is shaping up and how you can take advantage of market changes.

Sales is a dynamic discipline that evolves over time. By taking action and continuously improving your skills, you'll boost your sales performance and contribute to the ever-evolving art and science of sales.

7
CHAPTER

Accept Change and Adapt

There are several reasons why some companies never make it big in business. Many brilliant ideas do not succeed. A brilliant idea is just one thing, executing it brilliantly by a team of passionate members is equally important, if not more.

Many companies fail to plan effectively for their growth or expansion. Such organisations' growth depends on the brilliance of the one person who started the organisation. The founder goes through the ups and downs and survives because of their strong will and clarity of vision. When they start building a team, they look for people who will support them and not for people who will do things independently; hence, the desire to look for people who will be docile and willing to comply with directions is essential for many of them.

Why Loyalty becomes more important

Ajay ran a trading company and did reasonably well. In a business exchange program, I asked him why small organisations gave more preference to loyalty than smart work and why the doomsday theory was very strongly active in most small and mid-sized organisations, which made them bypass merit.

He explained the dilemma of the business owners while talking about his own experience. He used to run a small business selling technology products before. The team that worked with him decided to move away one day, taking the business with them. They had the customers and relationships, and they knew the methods of selling those technology solutions.

After working and building a team for three years, he was left stranded. He felt lost and had nothing to do. That day, he learnt an important lesson: You have to build a safety net within the limited size of the organisation. The system should help manage such uncertainties. Depending on few individuals is a necessity and a reality, however a business has to find still a way to survive and grow without fully depending on them.

How businesses can manage uncertainties

Focus on setting up systems and processes to help maintain control. The checks and balances can help control the damage of any misadventure. Do not underestimate the power of fear. It can force you to remain small and underdeveloped in the ways you manage your business. The Indian government did something similar in the Northeast. A road in the border area would give the Chinese Army free rein, so they did not develop it for 70 years. However, this strategy did not help us in the 1962 war. Still, we continued with the same strategy. We usually do the same in business. We refuse to learn, and we refuse to change.

If you cannot make radical changes in the system to grow the business, make incremental changes and be in touch with your team members and customers. Reduce dependence on individuals and build systems to run the operations. This is the best way to reduce uncertainties in small and mid-sized businesses

How to manage finance in a dynamic world

Lack of financial discipline is one big issue for poor growth of business. Let's illustrate this with an instance. I once briefly met with one of the finance directors of an organisation who had gone through a bad patch in his previous company and had to sell it off.

I asked him why small and mid-sized organisations have financial issues as a common problem. He explained that in such organisations, every expense looked justified. Hence, they found it challenging to control costs. Irrespective of their earnings, spending kept growing at a constant pace.

If revenue did not grow at the same pace, they took out loans and hoped that one day, they would see exponential growth and be able to pay off the outstanding loan amount. Unfortunately, that day never came, and the organisation collapsed.

He explained that they could avoid this situation in his new venture by controlling expenses. They spent only when it was necessary, otherwise saved money, and invested in assets whenever they had a windfall gain. Spending was always pessimistic until they got someone to fund the venture. However, even then, they did not go for extravagant expenditure. Initially, they avoided fancy offices, travel by business class, and parties in favour of necessities. No compromise on the necessities like having a sales team or travel expenses of the sales team was made. There is no one secret sauce for managing finance, so find your own and ensure that you do not go out of cash and go bust.

Adapt to changing dynamics

The business world constantly evolves, and successful companies adapt to change. Keep an eye on industry trends and stay ahead by innovating and taking calculated risks.

Newgen Software started as a document management company in 1992. The concept was a bit ahead of the time for India then. They were working on imaging technology and its usage in managing documents when they saw an opportunity to get into the creation of voter ID cards. They picked up this assignment by working with the government and sent a team nationwide to capture data and images and create voter ID cards. Many other vendors also jumped into it.

Newgen used its imaging technology and did an excellent job completing it on time. This did help them in investing more in their regular business. Today, *Newgen Software* is among the very few successful Indian software product companies from India, with customers in 70-plus countries.

In 1988, *Softek*, the Indian software product company, made compilers like *Basic, Cobol, Pascal*, etc. They found that the government wanted to work in bilingual mode and not just in English. The government also had a Hindi law with a parliamentary committee supporting it, but as no option was available to use Hindi on personal computers, no action was taken.

Section 3(3) of the Official Languages Act 1963 stated that all government offices should use the bilingual mode of communication or else the parliamentary committee can take suitable action. CDAC, the government organisation involved in IT research and development those days, had started working on a hardware solution to transliterate everything written in English to Hindi.

Softek thought of developing a Hindi word processor and database instead, which can work independently. In 1989, they came out with *Akshar*, the first bilingual word processor in the country. This worked in English and Hindi. This worked on compatible PCs. It was an instant hit. They started selling *Akshar* and *devBASE* (a bilingual database) like hotcakes.

Softek found a gap in the market and acted on it. Customers are the lifeline of any business, so stay focused on their needs and preferences. Listen to their feedback, adapt your products and services accordingly, and always be willing to go the extra mile to exceed their expectations. S*oftek* had a sales team operating out of all the five metro cities of India, who could take the product to the relevant customers. Many organizations have the product but do not have the right sales team to take it to the market. They usually have a sad ending.

Companies that cannot adapt to changing market conditions, customer needs, or technological advancements may not remain competitive in the long run. After a big business house took over *Softek*, all development work on the compilers, databases, and office productivity software almost reached a standstill. Instead of becoming the next *Microsoft* from India, they evaporated. They do not exist as a product company anymore. Most may not even know about them. This is what happens when innovation stops. This is what happens when you refuse to notice the shift in the market.

WordPerfect was the most popular word processor at one point in time. It controlled not only the Indian market but also the global market. However, they refused to change and adapt when the Windows operating system started catching up. Their word processor kept working on the MS-DOS environment. They slowly kept losing market to *Microsoft Word* on Windows environment but did not see the writing on the wall. They believed that Windows OS would continue the struggle and not replace the MS-DOS operating system soon. Overconfidence can kill and that is what happened precisely for *WordPerfect*. The leading word processor in the world market vanished.

Such things happen partly because of arrogance and poor leadership, and partly because of refusal to see the changing market dynamics. They do not try to set the system right; they refuse to listen to the customer-facing team's feedback. Customers do not usually switch to competition in a day; the exit is slow, and all the while, organisations have enough time to change and adapt.

Learning from history
Looking back at the history of the IT industry in India can help us get some perspective. In 1987, I joined the IT industry. *Microsoft*, *IBM*, and other international giants had no direct local presence. Bangalore and Chennai were sleepy cities with little IT presence. Most Indian personal computer manufacturers were based out of Delhi and Mumbai, with some exceptions like *Siva Computers* and *Wipro*, based out of Chennai and Bangalore respectively.

Organisations that had a bigger sales team made more sales. In some way, the organisation's sales were directly linked to the size of the its sales team. Most of them did not invest in innovation compared to the foreign players entering the Indian market. Organisations like *HCL*, *PCL*, *Wipro*, and *Siva* spent money on advertising and setting up a partner ecosystem to help them sell. So, they did well up to a point, i.e. until they did not face competition from international giants.

There was one Indian company that tried to sell its computer hardware in the USA and miserably failed. After that, came the second phase, when successful US companies started entering the Indian market. They usually had flashy offices and expensive products. They struggled in the price-sensitive Indian market in the beginning. They then focussed on building a solid partner network, did market segmentation depending on various factors, and helped grow the market. Customer behaviour started changing. Even in the home segment, customers paid a premium to buy foreign brands like *Compaq*, *IBM*, *HP*, etc. Customers liked the quality of the product and the prestige associated with it; customers agreed to pay a premium. The Indian companies refused to change. They kept justifying to themselves why they would still thrive and how their customers would keep coming back to them.

Lowering the price alone may not work
Some went into the low-price sales model, assuming low prices would be the game changer. The model did work in the initial phase. A massive media campaign did help some of them to book many orders, which was beyond their logistical capability. Strange things happened. People got delivery of boxes but did not know how to install the computer; hence, they had to wait. The installation engineer reached the location after a month or two with the computer since the already delivered boxes were actually empty! In those days, we believed that to be a smart move when such moves were disastrous for the organisation. Customers were losing trust and faith and were looking for an opportunity to move out. Lowering the price would have worked if they had managed their logistics better.

When faced with stiff competition from international vendors, the big brand names in the PC business in this country had to wind up their businesses. Many had been running their businesses successfully for 20 to 30 years but could not get geared up to face competition. The critical point is that they lost against the competition, which in most cases was selling a similar PC at a higher price.

Customers pay a premium even in price sensitive markets

People agreed to pay a 20 to 30 per cent premium in a price-sensitive country. Shocking but true. Many successful Indian IT product companies vanished. When I look back and think about how this happened, it is sometimes unbelievable that the market leaders could not survive the onslaught. The big question is has the IT industry learned from history?

Fortunately, the software services started picking up, and many could shift to that business. It was more lucrative, too, as India had a vast pool of IT resources getting trained in engineering colleges and IT training houses like NIIT and Aptech.

You can see a similarity with even ancient history here. We had kings and queens ruling us for centuries and then came foreign powers. We were not ready and were defeated on the battlefield. Many of these kings never had a strong army to defend their kingdoms. The alliances formed with neighbours were opportunistic; hence, under stress, they gave up. This happened multiple times in different locations of the country in different periods.

We will find similarities if we draw a parallel between the army with the sales teams of organisations. Many organisations do not have a strong sales team to defend against fierce competition from global giants. So, they lose market share but are happy as numerically they may still be growing, without knowing that they are losing hold over customers and no business can survive for long without adding new customers. Ultimately, only the global giants survive, and the local players shut shop and exit the market. They forget to keep checking the market share. They refuse to act.

In the same vein, we were doing great in the call centre business for a few years because we became the back office of the Western world and provided the same service at a lower cost. The companies should have done a risk analysis of every business unit every year, even in their heydays, but they did not.

Our only advantage was the availability of English speaking people at a lower cost. It was not much of a skill game. Slowly, some of our neighbouring countries with English speaking population also developed these skills and were ready to offer the same service at an even lesser cost. Gradually, all call centres vanished from India. The same is true for the medical transcription business.

Is price the only reason why customers change their vendors? What value addition could we have provided to make it difficult for competition to enter? Some Indian organisations set up centres in other parts of the world to take advantage of the price arbitrage. To evaluate lower price options, did we consider setting up centres in second-tier cities, the state capitals? The learning is to examine how your products and services might be affected by competition. What steps are you initiating to manage competition?

Planning and execution of the plan

Our biggest weakness in business houses is that we, with all our wisdom, become too creative in our planning and too weak in the execution of the plan. Ultimately, in many cases, what we plan and get as a result of our execution of the plan are two different things. This happens when too many people start changing on the fly at a strategy level.

Communicating the growth plan and ensuring that everyone is part of one organisation-wide strategy is usually missing. Everyone follows their instincts and does things according to what they understand. It can lead to chaos and unwelcome office politics.

The situation is similar to that of a chariot, where all horses start pulling in different directions instead of running in one direction. Your most significant strength of having multiple horses attached to the chariot becomes your biggest weakness. This is one big reason we have few successful billion-dollar sales organisations. Not just valuation; real numbers matter.

In a chariot with multiple horses, each horse represents a different aspect of a business. When these 'horses' pull in different directions, it signifies a lack of alignment within the organisation. This lack of alignment can lead to inefficiency, resource wastage, communication challenges, inconsistence customer experiences and limited success.

Similarly, it's important to note that in many cases, the valuation of an organisation is based not on its actual performance but on perceived performance potential. This can create a false sense of achievement, as high valuation doesn't always reflect the tangible, real-world results an organisation can deliver.

Organisations must work cohesively towards a common goal to achieve genuine success, aligning their efforts and resources to move in the same direction. This alignment is crucial for achieving substantial and sustainable growth in valuation and actual, measurable results.

8
CHAPTER

Unlocking Growth

Just as a gardener nurtures a young seedling into a thriving tree, fostering growth requires careful planning, adaptability, and a clear vision for the future. Whether it be personal development, professional success, or organisational advancement, the journey toward growth demands a proactive approach, a willingness to learn, and the cultivation of a growth mindset. By recognising the potential for growth and laying the groundwork for its fruition, individuals and entities can unlock their fullest potential and embrace a future of prosperity and achievement.

So, how does an organisation prepare for driving growth? What is it that they should do?

Solve a problem

First, the problem must exist, and people should be a bit desperate for a solution for it. So, if you sell something, try talking to your customers and understanding their concerns before imposing your ideas on them.

Understand how they are solving that problem now. What concerns do they have about that solution? How widespread is the need? Fill those gaps with your solution. Prepare a sales pitch to help communicate how you are solving the problem.

It was mandatory for every PC to have an operating system along with it at the time of shipping it. The locally assembled PC businesses were finding it expensive to add a copy of *Microsoft* Windows. They needed a low-cost alternative. At *ELX Linux* we decided to take advantage of this. We took our desktop version, which was recognised as the top Linux desktop in those times, and offered it at a throwaway price to some of the organisations. The price was such that the assemblers were finding it difficult to say 'no' to our offer. This was the starting point of selling in big numbers in the country.

Use the product yourself

Before you go out to sell it, it is advisable to first use the product to know how it works, and why it works the way it works. Alternatively, have a small sample size to check and understand the potential customer behaviour and try to fix any glitches if they exist. Managing a small sample size is easy and will not have much negative impact, even if the product or solution does not do what it intends.

This will also help you understand the product's advantage and help iron out the basic level discomforts, if any. This can also help you get insight into the usage from a real user's perspective and that can play an important role in making more sales.

At *ELX Linux* we asked our sales and technical sales team to install the product on their desktop and use it for day-to-day activities. This helped in understanding and resolving the problems at a much faster pace. This also gave the needed confidence to the team. They were not just saying something, they were actually using it every day.

The helpdesk

Everyone knows about this but very few manage a helpdesk properly. What the Helpdesk lacks in many cases is a qualified team with the needed authority to address the customer's problems.

Depending on the nature of the product or service and the geography you cover, you should decide if you need to provide a 24/7 helpdesk or if a regular office-hour helpdesk will do. Track the turnaround time of solving a problem. Create a list of all issues and their solutions and put them in a way that other people in the helpdesk can refer to them and give quick resolutions in case the same problem gets repeated, which usually happens. This will help improve ticket resolution time in your helpdesk and will help win more customers for you.

Avoid overcommitting about the capacity and capability of your helpdesk. If you cannot provide a 24/7 helpdesk, then avoid committing it. Help customers through online forums in such cases where even customers can respond, and your team, whenever they have time, can respond.

At *Newgen*, the Channel/Partner team created a virtual helpdesk where they uploaded more than 3,000 queries with probable solutions and made it available to 350 plus partners spread across 70 countries. The partners can log in at any point of time and check for answers. Only those problems which they were not able to solve using the virtual helpdesk, were being forwarded to the Partner Support Centre for help. This helped reduce the number of problems which needed individual attention and also helped them maintain a turnaround time of 72 hours for 90% of the queries.

Define standard operating procedures for managing sales

From when you decide to go into the market to sell a product to the time the customer buys and starts using the product, there should be a pre-defined and well-oiled sales and support process. It must work, and it must do so every time. So, step one is to list all possible factors that will influence or impact the sales process, the next is to see how those factors can be put in a way where implementing the strategy and improvising the process at a later date if needed becomes easy or at least possible.

At *IBM,* I managed the volume business of software for India/South Asia. There was a team that used to help in lead generation. The partner management team ensured we had enough partners across the geography to help us. They also worked with the distributor to ensure that all payments issues with the partners are managed by the distributor and IBM gets its payment in defined time period always. The technical support team used to jump in for any discussion which the sales team was not able to manage. There was a large inside sales team and a comparatively smaller field sales team. The inside sales team had specialists and worked with those customers who were buying products or solutions which met their specialised product suites. The field sales team were generalists and they knew something about everything. The marketing team use to run marketing activities like customer events and webinars to help progress leads.

Overall, it worked like a big war machine. Everyone was doing a different activity but trying to achieve the common goal of driving a sales number. Teams were loosely coupled, hence some of the teams worked for other teams too without impacting any team's work. We were closing multiple deals every week, adding more new customers and gaining market share.

Audit the system regularly

Ensure that your systems are relevant and that the SOP (standard operating procedure) is not only on paper but working on the ground. Check if the system is helping the organisation grow the business, or else one needs to look into the system and look for bottlenecks. A good system alone is not enough; it should be implemented correctly so that it helps you grow the business with minimum injustice to the sincere and dedicated workers. A flawed system is terrible for good employees.

Organisations usually have internal auditors to do a review regularly and raise red flag when they see a problem with any financial transaction. This helps in avoiding any financial disaster. Similarly, businesses should have a business audit regularly by third party who will not be afraid to tell the truth to the leadership. They should review all the possible business processes in regular interval by talking to people in different departments and submit a report. People will give honest feedback only if they know that their career will not get impacted by speaking the truth.

This will help you manage and grow your business much better and faster.

Avoid shortcuts

Shortcuts are stop-gap arrangements and should only be used as such. Unfortunately, that stop-gap becomes a permanent solution, and that is when we start faltering. Try doing things right even if it takes longer and costs more money. In the end, your pace of growth and success will depend on that. We have developed a habit of getting too impressed by 'shortcuts' and do not see the pitfalls because of this.

Avoid a single point of failure

We need to avoid a single point of failure. If one person or team fails or has a chance of failure, the other team should be able to point it out and help rectify the situation before it is too late. This should be part of the system and should be designed and implemented so that people do not start intruding or interfering in the work of other teams. This will help ensure corrective steps are taken before it is too late.

Let us take an example of a sales organisation that wants to introduce a new product, say mail messaging software, in the market. A brand person can be given the target to drive sales of that product including the creation of the sales kit.

The sales team will sell what they think they can sell to achieve their targets, so the brand needs to create an environment where the sales see value in pushing the mail messaging software.

The Channel Sales team will create, train, and nurture the ecosystem based on the organisation's expectations. As this expectation aligns with what the brand or sales team is expected to do, the brand team will try to promote the ecosystem partners who show interest. Marketing will run campaigns to help create pull for the product in the same market segment. All this will ensure that the market starts taking an interest in the product resulting in sales.

If the product does not do what it is expected to do, or, feature-wise and usage-wise the customer expects much more for the price charged, the feedback should go back to the product team and they should be informed about the changed market demands.

This means that only the sales team does not define the product's success, and similarly, the product will not fail just because one team or leader failed. This is what avoiding a single point of failure is all about. Depending on the nature of the business you are in, one has to decide how it will work on the ground to avoid getting surprises as much as possible.

9

CHAPTER

Affordable Pricing and Sales Cycle

Designing an effective, affordable pricing strategy for a product or service can significantly impact its success in the market. This affects the customer's perception of value and the company's profitability. There is an art to pricing.

Pricing for complex solutions can also be perceived as intimidating, even if they bring significant value. This is where effective communication and marketing strategies come into play to help potential customers understand the value proposition and benefits of the solutions so they do not hesitate to decide. Organisations can break one complex price into optional and not optional multiple prices to help customers start small if they wish. It will allow the organisation to have a bigger footprint.

In addition to using customer feedback and testimonials to highlight the value of their solutions, businesses can also use them to highlight the positive experiences that others have had with them. This can help alleviate any concerns or doubts that potential customers may have about the solutions and increase their willingness to purchase. Established players' pricing can teach you much about pricing but cannot be used to price your product.

Pricing and discounting work better for known brand names and do not give the same advantage if you sell an unknown brand. The perceived value of unknown products is lacking, so discounting does not have the desired impact.

Crafting your unique value

The secret sauce for pricing power is the art of crafting a unique value proposition that not only sets your product or service apart but also empowers you to command higher prices. You need to discover how to make your offering stand out in a crowded marketplace and even entice customers to pay a premium.

Look at some online stores like *Fresh to Home* or *Big Basket.* They sell standard products like fish, chicken or fruits and vegetables at a premium. There is a big market for those basic level products at a premium, depending on the quality, availability, and dependability of service.

Most of these products are available in your neighbourhood stores at a price point that is much cheaper than the online stores. This proves that people will pay more if you can create unique value.

Communicating value through price

The more unique and valuable your product or service is, the higher the price you can charge provided you are able to communicate the same to the potential customers.

Look at the pricing of *iPhone* and *iPad* compared to their competition. Many offer almost similar products at half the price and struggle to sell. The same is true for many other products. Crafting your unique value helps to ask for a premium.

Consider offering discounts or promotions to attract customers. Organisations that come up with a new version or model tend to sell the older version at a lower price, and in some cases where there is no inventory cost, you may like to look at it differently. The previous version of the software, at a lower cost, can eat into your current market alternatively, it may also help you win in that marketplace where customers want fewer features but need a similar product. You can block competition by selling the older version at a lower price.

Some organisations cannibalise their products by pricing the new model or version at a lower cost, discouraging people from buying the older version. This also ensures that people do not go to the competition.

Pricing strategies unveiled

To find the winning formula, explore the fascinating world of pricing strategies tailored to your specific sales approach. From cost-plus pricing for services to penetration pricing that undercuts the competition, you can unravel the mysteries of strategic pricing. Learn when to use each strategy and how to balance profitability and market dominance.

Establishing a pricing strategy will be dependent on your sales plan. You need to charge cost-plus if it's a service you're selling. If you want to enter a competitive market, you may like to follow penetration pricing by undercutting your competition and backing it up with the needed marketing effort. However, keep a check on the duration of such a campaign, or it may force you to go bankrupt. Alternatively, you can have an entry price with fewer features at a heavy discount to entice customers to try your product and a premium price for those who demand more value. Make the premium look premium by adding many extras, and ensure you honour more than you commit.

Let us take the example of the pricing of packaged water. Water is water, and around 10,000 registered vendors are selling packaged water in India. So why is it that when the end product is the same; some charge more and yet do huge amounts of business and are highly profitable, and some charge low and somehow manage to survive? You will get business houses claiming their water tastes better, but how many people drink water because of taste? It should primarily quench the thirst and should not taste awful.

The packaged water market in India can be complex and competitive, with many registered vendors offering similar products. Pricing in this market can vary widely based on factors such as value addition, distribution, availability, brand reputation, and marketing efforts.

Distribution and availability play an important role. One can have their own offices or use partners to distribute, as distribution can be a significant challenge. There may be a high demand for packaged water in under-served markets, where there are few vendors and limited access to clean drinking water. In contrast, in well-served markets, where supply is abundant by multiple vendors, competition can be fierce, and prices may be more competitive.

The factor influencing pricing is the vendor's brand reputation and marketing efforts. Established brands with a strong reputation for quality and safety can command a higher price for their products. At the same time, smaller or less well-known vendors may need to compete on price to attract customers irrespective of the superior quality they offer.

Innovative price strategy

Another example of smart pricing can be beverage shops in many parts of the globe. They offer three-tier pricing and tempt the customers to spend more. By offering three price tiers (small, medium, and large), businesses can create a sense of value for customers considering the medium option. Since the large option is only marginally more expensive than the medium option, customers may be inclined to choose it because they feel they are getting more value.

Similarly, one can offer a new product for free or at a throwaway price along with some fast-selling product. This helps you get your product inside the customer inventory, hoping they will use it and buy more. Organisations also use this method to plant their product in multiple organisations and claim a significant user base, as many customers do not want to be the first user. So, the introductory price of a completely new product can be kept hidden for some time. One can test the market in the garb of giving something for free to a loyal customer and then decide on the pricing.

Test and refine

After implementing your pricing strategy, track its effectiveness by analysing sales data and customer feedback. You may need to adjust based on the results to optimise your pricing strategy. Do not hesitate to return to the drawing board and rework the pricing strategy if needed. The sole purpose of this should be to increase sales revenue.

Remember, pricing is not a one-time event but an ongoing process that should be evaluated regularly to ensure you maximise profits and meet customer needs. One should also look at the marketing expense needed to give the product visibility, which should help you achieve the needed volume. Everything comes at a cost, and they need to be part of your pricing strategy. For example, apart from production cost, there are many other expenses. Inventory holding, warehouse, partner margin, and distribution costs can easily exceed 45% of your product MRP. If you do not make provision for such expenses, you can run out of cash and go bankrupt.

Sales cycle time

The sales cycle time can differ from 40 seconds to 40 months. The pricing will be impacted by the critical need of the product, competition, and the buyer's demand for it. Lower cost can be the game changer if you are looking at the mass market and quick turnaround time. If you can establish trust, you can sell the same thing at a higher price, too, and it will be acceptable. However, establishing trust can be time-consuming and impact your revenue in the short run.

Time vs. utility in pricing

A bad product can be sold at a low price for a long time if the buyers see its value, such as Chinese toys. They are cheap but also not of good quality. However, it would help if you had them to give it as a gift or even give it to your kids often. Knowing that these low-cost toys or products will not last long, people do not mind taking the risk of buying them. This is for two reasons primarily. One is that they do not see an alternative product available at that cost; second, they may need more budget for gifting better, which can be challenging; hence, these low-cost toys find preference. So, the utility of the product or service also determines what kind of pricing will be acceptable.

The time involved in selling a product or service may not always be directly related to the cost of the product or the solution. The speed of sale will also depend on awareness about the product, the need for the product, and the options available to the customer at the time of buying.

When people go to a shop to buy products available at a discounted price, it is assumed that people would rush the purchase. While a similar type of product in normal circumstances would take more time. Selling is largely driven by brand name recognition and the fear of losing a good deal. So, when *Meena Bazaar* offers a 50% discount sale on sarees, there can be a big rush to buy.

The seasonal impact of sales also can be big, provided you have done enough homework and have created a brand name for yourself. *Khadim* shoes in Kolkata sell like hotcakes before Durga Puja for two reasons. One is the cost, and the second is the established brand name for low-cost shoes. However, a less-known brand with a 50% discount may not attract any attention.

Market entry pricing

The simple way to look at the entry-level cost will depend on the market you are trying to address and the volume you are trying to attain. Many customers may assume that all low-cost products are bad and most high-value products are good.

Introductory pricing is commonly used to introduce a new product or service. When a new product is launched, it is only sometimes well-known to consumers, and it can be challenging to convince them to try it out, especially if it is priced too high.

To address this challenge, companies often use introductory pricing, which involves offering the new product at a lower price than its eventual regular price for a limited time. This reduced price incentivises potential customers to try the product and creates buzz around its launch. Typically, the price increases to its regular level after the introductory period.

When determining the introductory price, companies need to consider several factors, including their costs, the value proposition of the product, and the price sensitivity of their target market. The introductory price should be low enough to attract customers but high enough to generate revenue and not damage the brand's perceived value.

Overall, introductory pricing is a common strategy used to generate buzz and encourage the trial of a new product, mainly if it is not well-known or has no established market.

Bundle pricing

Offering bundles or packages of products or services at a discounted price can help you gain and retain market share by providing customers with more value for their money. This has become quite common in online portals. They tempt customers by bundling an additional product at an incremental cost. Customers sitting on the fence and not sure if they should buy the other product or not usually fall for this strategy and decide to buy.

Dynamic pricing

Dynamic pricing is where prices are adjusted, upwards or downwards, based on market demand and other factors. One can lose or gain and retain market share by allowing you to react quickly to changing market conditions and stay competitive. In such a situation, you have a defined list price; however, the sales price will depend on various other factors like competition, time of the year, need for more business, etc.

Ola or *Uber* taxi service is one example of working successfully globally. Similarly, perishable goods can be priced following this strategy. When they are fresh, you can charge high; you can drop the price when they are about to become stale. Even my book, *Lamb Leading Lions*, was dynamically priced. When the sales picked up, the prices on *Amazon* and *Flipkart* went up, and when the sales reduced, they dropped the prices.

Dynamic pricing holds good in most cases. However, there are exceptions to the rule where the big players do not allow the principle of dynamic pricing to work against their interests. Diamonds sold by unknown sellers are branded as conflict diamonds, and customers are discouraged from buying them on ethical grounds. According to them, conflict diamonds are sold by people who have got them through violence, and if you buy them, you encourage more violence. This helps control the uncertainty and ensures that the sudden inflow of diamonds in the market will not impact negatively.

Promotions and discounts

Offering promotions and discounts can help you gain and retain market share by incentivising customers to purchase or stay loyal to your brand.

It's important to note that pricing should be part of a larger strategy considering other marketing mix elements, such as product quality, distribution, and promotion. By strategically considering these factors and pricing, businesses can gain and retain market share, build brand loyalty, and achieve long-term success.

Discounting is a typical pricing strategy businesses use in competitive markets to attract price-sensitive customers and gain market share. Although, discounting can be an effective short-term strategy, it can also have some drawbacks if used excessively or without careful consideration.

Here are some things to keep in mind when discounting in a competitive market:

Have a clear strategy: Discounting can be effective in the short term, but it's essential to have a clear strategy for how and when you will offer discounts. Offering discounts too frequently can damage the perceived value of your product or service and create a perception that it's only worth buying when it's on sale.

Target the right customers: It's essential to target your discounting strategy to the right customers. Offering discounts to existing loyal customers can help build brand loyalty, while providing discounts to new customers can help attract them to your product or service.

Monitor competitor pricing: In a competitive market, monitoring your competitors' pricing and adjusting your discounting strategy accordingly is essential. If your competitors offer deep discounts, you may need to provide similar deals to remain competitive.

Do not rely solely on discounting: While discounting can be effective in the short term, it's essential to have a broader pricing strategy considering value-based pricing and product differentiation factors. Relying solely on discounting can create a perception that your product or service is only valuable when it's on sale, which can damage the long-term success of your business.

The art of irresistible bargains

Discover the dynamic world of deep discounting and how it can turn the tide in your favour. Mastering deep discounting is possible once you unlock the secrets of when, why, and how to wield deep discounts effectively. Uncover the psychology behind bargain hunting and learn how to use this powerful tool to boost sales, clear inventory, and win customer loyalty without compromising your brand's value.

Deep discounting is a pricing strategy in which a product or service is offered significantly lower than its regular price. It can be an effective way to drive sales and attract price-sensitive customers. Here are some situations when deep discounting may be appropriate:

Slow sales: Deep discounting can effectively clear inventory and generate revenue if a product or service is not selling well or moving slowly. This can also be useful for seasonal products that must be sold before the end of the season. Even when you decide to come out with a new version, it may make sense to come out with special pricing offers to clear the stock. In the software business, there can be customers who cannot afford your products because of price; you may consider selling the older versions at a lower cost for some time.

Clearing excess inventory: Deep discounting can effectively sell the inventory quickly and generate revenue if a business has excess inventory that needs to be cleared. This is particularly relevant for products with limited shelf life, or that will become outdated or less valuable.

Building customer loyalty: Offering deep discounts to existing customers can effectively build brand loyalty and retain customers. This strategy can also help to differentiate your brand from your competitors and make your customers feel valued.

Launching a new product: Offering deep discounts for a new product can be a way to generate buzz and encourage customers to try the product. This strategy can be particularly effective if the new product is similar to products offered by competitors but at a lower price.

Competing with rivals: If competitors offer deep discounts, businesses may need to follow suit to remain competitive. Deep discounting can effectively attract price-sensitive customers and gain market share.

Overall, deep discounting should be used carefully and strategically. While it can be an effective way to drive sales and attract customers, it can also erode profit margins and damage the perceived value of the product or service. It can threaten the survival of the organisation itself. It's crucial to carefully weigh the costs and benefits of deep discounting before implementing this pricing strategy.

Analyse your market, competition, and sales approach. Decide on the pricing strategy that best aligns with your business goals. Whether it's cost-plus pricing, penetration pricing, or something in between, ensure it resonates with your target audience. Ensure that your sales team understands the logic to convince their customers with utmost conviction.

10
CHAPTER

Stop Thinking Outside the Box

The Western world includes several countries with different weather patterns and conditions. Some regions have harsh weather conditions, such as extreme heat or cold, snowstorms, or hurricanes; others may have more moderate weather conditions. Severe weather can be deadly without proper preparation. In regions with extreme weather conditions, people have learned to adapt and develop a disciplined approach to dealing with these challenges.

People must plan for weather conditions, be it snowstorms or heatwaves, well in advance. This can mean being more regimented in their daily routines, such as ensuring they have enough food and water supplies or taking precautions when to venture outside. For instance, while driving on icy roads ensuring that the tyres have snow chains, that the heating system is working etc. as making mistakes can be life-threatening. This leads to a more disciplined lifestyle.

The consequences of violating rules can be severe. Any violation of the ground rules, therefore, was discouraged. For example, if people become adventurous and venture out in extreme cold without the needed preparation, they can get stranded where no help is available. A situation like this can mean death. A strict adherence to defined processes and systems resulted from this. Everything started happening based on defined procedures and processes. Creativity diminished, highlighting the need to encourage thinking outside the box.

Thinking 'inside the box'
In the western world, thinking 'inside the box' is conventional, relying on established ideas and practices. It involves following established guidelines or principles rather than finding new solutions or approaches. As systems

function, people avoid thinking differently, limiting creativity. People have no motivation to think differently than what is already defined.

Thinking 'outside the box' is a term used to describe the act of thinking creatively, innovatively, and unconventionally to solve problems or generate new ideas. It means looking beyond the usual or traditional ways of thinking and considering alternative perspectives or approaches.

The term 'box' refers to the limits or constraints that we often place on our thinking, either consciously or unconsciously, due to our experiences, assumptions, biases, or the rules and norms of the environment where we live. To think outside the box, one must break free from these constraints and explore new possibilities and solutions.

The belief is that thinking outside the box can lead to breakthroughs and paradigm shifts, especially in fields that require innovation and originality, such as science, technology, art, and business. It requires an open and flexible mindset, a willingness to take risks, experiment, and challenge the status quo, and a capacity for divergent thinking and creative problem-solving.

So, why should we stop thinking outside the box?

This suggestion is more for people born and raised outside the West. The lack of resources and struggle for everyday things makes us improvise in everything. We do this in the quest for better solutions, which often leads to more chaos and, at times, to reasonable solutions.

Impact of weather on behaviour

Our weather is neither extreme nor harsh, barring the desert region in the west and snowy mountains of the north. We can and do survive even if we do not follow strict guidelines. The slightly warm and humid weather in the country's eastern region provides in abundance and makes the behaviour of inhabitants lazy and slow. It has changed their behaviour and made them more creative than people in other parts of the country. The dry heat and extreme cold in the North encourage outdoor activities, leading to a more assertive and physically active community. Conversely, in the South, the combination of varied weather patterns results in a mix of individuals who display both high levels of aggression and creativity, reflecting the nuanced impact of climatic influences on the behaviour of the Indian population as a whole.

This typical weather condition has conditioned our minds to behave accordingly; hence, we have become less regimental, and more mystic and creative. Survival was never an issue. Neither doing things right in the first go was a priority. Hence, we developed different ways of looking at and solving a problem. An improvisation that will resolve the current issue without solving the core problem once and for all became a habit. Which meant we encouraged the behaviour of improvisation at every level.

Impact of instant improvisation

Without enough depth and knowledge, these improvisations can mean developing poor-quality products and solutions. In the pre-1990 era, we lived in a closed economy with not enough options to choose from. Hence, we developed a fundamental nature of accepting products and solutions which were not perfect. Masses did not have many options to choose from.

So, we improvised whenever we were in trouble or found that something was not getting the given job done. On-the-fly improvisation bailed us out temporarily but slowly became a norm, a kind of habit. However, we never spent enough time and resources, even when we had them, to create quality products at an economical price.

Look at air coolers, non-stick cooking material, shoes, or anything else. One is never sure of the quality of the locally made products in our country; hence, people prefer to buy from an organisation known for quality products or services if they have the financial capacity to pay. Sometimes, they end up paying 100 per cent more just to be sure that the product will do what it claims. The market is big and has a potential for all kinds of products; hence, many products and service organisations survive even when what they do is not of good quality. However, they only survive and do not excel.

Many organisations start developing their products or services with the dream that they would produce things which people can rely upon and buy. However, they agree to compromise and go for a make-shift arrangement when they face an issue with the material, technology, or skills. If the arrangement looks good, they do not change it until they are forced to. They are happy with the ad-hoc changes made by their team to get things working. Ad-hoc improvisation looks good initially, and slowly, in many cases, that becomes the reason for failure or a bigger problem.

In a housing society, a new flat owner was finishing the interior work and part of the deal was also to fix the old wiring. The electrician did the work with one improvisation. As he found the electricity tripping daily, causing inconvenience, he took out the safety mechanism. He bypassed the safety mechanism and connected it directly to the electric meter without understanding why it was tripping. The new owner stopped complaining after the tripping stopped. It looked like a good instant solution.

Then, one day, the inevitable happened. The meter caught fire because of overloading. The safety system was taken out without understanding the reason for the problem. The electricity department was upset with this and penalised the new owner. So, the new owner ended up paying a penalty, apart from the cost of the burnt meter and the harassment for the next three days.

This is what happens with such quick-fix solutions, primarily improvisation, without much thought in many cases. As the solution provider fixes the problem temporarily, no serious effort is put into long-term solutions. Thus, while thinking outside the box at every point does help solve problems temporarily, it also causes a significant issue later in many cases. Most do not learn from such experiences.

Why the world should stop thinking outside the box

About 80 per cent of the world lacks predefined systems. This leads to the habit of not following processes. Hence, everyone does what they think is right. Sometimes, this outcome is good, and at other times, it is disastrous. The above instance of an electrician solving a problem is an example which illustrates this.

So, when people are forced to think inside the box and work in a controlled manner, they will make fewer mistakes as they will not be trying something new or different every time. Thinking inside the box in 80 per cent of the world can benefit them and hence, should be encouraged. A balanced thinking approach can benefit the masses in day-to-day affairs in their own life and help run business organisations more effectively.

In countries where people struggle in everyday life to carry out any given activity, like reaching the office in time by taking the same route, returning a product if it does not do what it promises, or getting your kid admitted to a good school, etc. they are always thinking of ways to manage the situation as standard processes are either not available or do not work. In all such countries, one should teach people not to think and follow the defined instructions while working in an organisation. As a result, everyone will follow instructions precisely.

If any issue or error is found, it can be rectified for everyone. This will help you execute more successful projects even in your daily life. Behaviour like this will simplify the job of training your sales team, partner network, and external vendors working with you. This will also ensure the successful implementation of ideas. Good ideas are a concern in most of the world, but implementing them effectively in the defined time is a bigger problem.

For example, suppose you roll out a global selling strategy that states that the market should be divided into small deals of less than one crore rupees (USD 120,000). In that case, the latter will be handled by one team, while another group will handle all deals of higher value than a crore dubbed the large deals team. In a systems-driven organisation, this will work every time for every deal across the globe; however, if the sales team starts interpreting it differently and starts being creative with it, they can find ways of manipulating the system. They can go after a deal of two crores value and give an extra discount and call it a less than one crore deal to take credit for the deal.

Similarly, the other team can come back and say that the potential of doing business in a given organisation over the next few years is two crores (US$240,000); hence, it should be part of the large deals, even if the order value is less than ₹50 lacs (USD 60,000). This will mean endless disputes. The teams will be too busy manipulating the system to do their jobs, creating more confusion and less business.

Implications of improvisation on the fly

When systems and processes do not always work, people tend to find a creative way to make things happen. As a result, employees are used to improvising on every task. This is more out of habit. There is a lack of respect for defined systems in many cases. In India, people have also given a name to this '*jugaad*'. This means improvisation on the fly. A different type of challenge arises as a result. You start with one objective and one methodology to achieve that objective; however, during implementation, the constant improvisation changes the approach so much that it can lead to system failure and non-achievement. This improvisation can lead to great results also in some places. Hence, such improvisations are encouraged and have become a norm.

Now, at a central place, if you are trying to monitor the rollout of any program which is getting improvised on the fly based on the respective people on the ground, then the one sitting at the head office may never come to know why a given rollout flopped in one place and succeeded in another. Hence, when rolled out on a large scale, any project becomes challenging to manage.

So, why has this culture of *jugaad* or 'instant improvisation' taken deep root in our society?

There is always a lack of skilled people and needed resources; hence, if you define a system that mentions and strictly follows how many people with what skills and resources are needed to execute any given task, many tasks may never even begin. Everyone suffers. However, the concept of *jugaad* has ensured that complex activities, even without needed knowledge or specialisation, can be attempted as nothing is supposed to be impossible, and almost everyone can attempt everything. This has ensured that life keeps moving, with or without resources. You need people who have the courage to try and improvise.

Now, if *jugaad* is so beneficial, why do we need to stop thinking outside the box, and why do we need to get out of this concept?

Why defining a process is helpful

Defined processes always help as everyone is aware of what is expected out of them and out of others. Surprises are minimal. Hence, people do not waste time thinking of possible alternatives in everything; they can focus on their work and become more productive. People responsible for thinking will do the thinking.

This also means that until the product delivers perfect results, one will keep working on it in the lab environment and only release the product in the market when they are sure of the quality and the functionality. This is the first step towards releasing quality products. You need this in every manufacturing or product development business to start with. This leads to happier customers and, consequently, business growth. Making quality work a habit can be a game changer for business.

Conclusion

In the western world, things are more process-based. These process-based societies impact the creativity of the individual. The need to think creatively to survive every day ordeal does not exist. It is therefore, necessary to let them know they are expected to think. Hence, there is the need to ask them to think 'outside the box'.

In contrast, the rest of the world should be taught how important it is to think 'inside the box'. Why it is crucial to follow defined rules and systems and why too many ideas and too many improvisations on the ground by too many people can be bad for the execution of any strategy and bad for business.

11
CHAPTER

Build the War Machine

The global business landscape evolves rapidly, with new entrants and exits. Organisations must adapt to the dynamics of markets to succeed. There is a need for both innovation and adaptation if they want to build a strong war machine which can deliver performance and growth.

Organisations need to innovate to stay ahead of themselves and the competition. This means that organisations must invest in the right people and technology. They must develop a strong culture that combines a process-driven approach with space for creativity and continuous improvement. Where you start may not be that important, but how you progress and manage growth to reach the ultimate objective can be the real acid test.

Empower teams to work towards common objectives. Let the teams build their plan to help achieve that common objective aligned with the broad strategy. The most crucial element is to have effective communication from the top and prevent any conflicts. All energy should be focused towards growth.

Effective communication
The CEO should first communicate their key result areas (KRAs) and strategy. Departments should pick their part from that strategy and create their unit plan.

You should have a defined and well-documented strategy document easy to understand and follow with realistic goals. Encourage people to follow that for sales, marketing, product development, and territory definition. In order to engage internally with teams, and externally with partners and customers, having a defined strategy that everyone will know and follow is a must. People should not be encouraged to improvise the strategy on the fly while executing the same. The broad parameters should be such that the interpretation of the document should not mean different things to different people and it must be sacrosanct so everyone is on the same page. The departments cannot change the strategy, but the tactics can be revised.

Build a war machine in a way so that different departments, whether big or small, in the same city or spread across different countries, should have a defined way of working, and everyone should follow the same rules of engagement. This will mean that people do not have to keep guessing about the other team members' moves and how different teams will align and deliver. They all will broadly know under which circumstances what is expected and how they will react. This will increase reaction time and help stop inefficiency in the system as multiple people and teams will be looking at the system and be able to comment or participate in fixing the issues.

In the 90s, as a Branch Manager in Kolkata, my daily routine was burdened with administrative tasks despite sales being the primary focus. This is an illustration of how poor systems force sales leaders to waste their time and energy in solving everyday basic issues.

In the first month of my joining, I discovered that petty cash was never enough to manage the day-to-day expenditures. The leadership at the head office were not very keen on solving these issues either, as they thought the right way of managing branch expenses was by slashing asks by 50%. This meant spending too much time and energy solving petty cash issues in the office rather than helping teams do more business. Hiring resources was the next big issue. Getting a person onboarded was always like a puzzle-solving game. As unnecessary delays impacted working, we hired whomever we could. So, we usually compromised on the salary and compromised on the candidate.

Opening branch offices without going through due diligence can have disturbing consequences. All this will mean weak branch office performance. This impacts overall revenue and in turn, growth.

Addressing departmental challenges

Specific departments may receive more privileges than others. Some leaders are better than others in asking for money and resources hence they get it and some suffer. Defining systems and processes that are not personality-based can help resolve such issues. Another way to partially resolve this issue is by regularly rotating the heads of the departments. The rotations need not occur at fixed intervals but should be done to ensure that each head understands the concerns and challenges of every department. This will help them improve the overall functioning of the organisation. Knowing they could be asked to manage any department, leaders strive to prevent departmental injustices.

Focus should be growth and this will be only possible when everyone focusses towards building the war machine.

One morning, the Personnel Manager of the Jute Mill in Kankinara, West Bengal, came rushing to the office of the General Manager. He was upset.

Personnel Manager (PM): Sir, the labour union is very upset, and some leaders came shouting at my office a few minutes back. I narrowly escaped getting beaten up.

General Manager (GM): Why are they upset? What is their demand now?

PM: Sir, the workers' toilet is overflowing and stinking. The situation of their toilet is usually bad, but this time it is too bad.

GM: Have they complained to the department concerned?

PM: I have complained to maintenance twice in the last few days. Nothing has changed. They have a staff shortage, so they want us to give them more time. The Maintenance Manager is least bothered about our problem. However, the Union is getting restless now. Can you please intervene and help?

GM: Okay, do one thing. Allow the labourers to use the officer's toilet until theirs get repaired and cleaned.

PM (Flabbergasted at the reply): Are you sure you want us to do this?

GM: Do you have a better idea? I am sure with this change by evening, everything will get resolved, and the labourers toilet will be spic and span for use. Let the officers decide, including yourself, how much time they need to solve this.

As predicted by the General Manager, everything was resolved in the next few hours. Something that was pending for weeks got resolved within a few hours.

People generally do not bother about the other person's problem until they face it themselves. Knowing very well that a worker's problem is the organisation's problem and a poor work environment for the worker will impact production and productivity, organisations do not attempt to improve things. So, help the leaders learn to appreciate other people's problems too, let them learn to be better team players.

In the same way, no sales team will succeed if you do not have the right work environment. Leaders should be willing to help each other and that will reduce unwanted friction and improve your chances of selling more.

To succeed in sales, define your organisation's structure just as a well-organised military structure. It includes infantry, artillery, paratroopers, and air support. Infantry leads ground combat, artillery offers long-range fire support, paratroopers disrupt behind enemy lines, and air support dominates the sky, aiding ground troops for battlefield victory. Similarly, success in sales requires a multidimensional approach, and it's essential to have a team that can work together towards a common goal.

Organisations must choose sales strategies based on their size, industry, target market, and goals. Traditionally, people follow a few standard selling methods, and some of them have been explained below for better understanding.

Different type of sales teams

Direct Sales: Involves sales teams who directly engages with potential customers. The cost of managing such a team will be high.

Channel Sales: Organisations collaborate with partners like resellers or distributors to reach broader audiences and access new markets. This also helps reduce the cost of maintaining your big sales team.

E-Commerce Sales: This approach involves selling products or services through an online platform, such as a website or marketplace. Online sales can be a practical approach for organisations with a large customer base and a product or service that can be quickly sold online.

Organisations must evaluate their options and choose a sales approach that aligns with their strengths and objectives.

Specialised teams

Brand leaders: A strong brand boosts loyalty, recognition, and revenue. They should understand team needs, monitor competition, and drive brand growth. Brand managers collaborate with sales, partners, and product development, enhancing market appeal and enabling sales. They should carry the overall brand sales number and should run with the sales teams to drive revenue.

Special initiative team: Introducing a new product in the market may need special initiatives for a limited time. In 2005, I joined *IBM* to spearhead the Linux software sales initiative in India, aiming for a specific share of *IBM* software business on Linux OS. With a four-person technical team, I supported internal teams, partners, and customers adopting Linux. After achieving our goal, the initiative team merged with other sales teams.

Loyalty program team: A loyalty program can effectively retain existing customers and incentivise repeat purchases. It could include discounts, exclusive offers, or other perks. Organisations can maintain all existing customers' details and automatically give special pricing offers for repeat customers. So, one can define that someone who buys a product more than twice or of a value will get a standard discount of X percentage whenever they buy next. Customers appreciate this gesture. Many global product companies follow this as part of their overall strategy to acquire and retain customers.

Special category programs can also be launched to promote a given segment. So, one can decide on a special offer for the government customer. Similarly, special offers can be worked out for educational institutions or NGOs. This will encourage the adoption of your product line by the special category customers who may be unable to procure the product otherwise.

Encouraging existing customers to refer other customers or their friends and family can help increase your customer base for all products and services. Offer referral incentives, such as discounts, free products, or an invitation for an evening out with similar customers. Use customer references like email or video referrals to communicate with other customers.

There are instances where organisations may have taken certain actions that were not part of their overall strategy but were done as a special case. If these actions have proven to be successful, it may be worthwhile to incorporate them as part of the annual strategy. Businesses can see the positive impact these actions can have on their overall success by dedicating the necessary resources.

Strategic partnerships team

Partnerships with other businesses, which can complement and sometimes compete, can help expand your customer base and reach new markets. Look for complementary businesses with a similar target audience to partner with. Approach such meetings with an open mind as the strategic partner may have other interests which can be conflicting in some cases. Hence, instead of only looking for your benefits from a relationship, try to address the interests and concerns of the strategic partners, too, so that the partnership lasts longer and both parties gain.

Look at the partnership between the *Maruti Suzuki Baleno* and *Toyota Glanza*. *Maruti Suzuki* engineered the car, and *Toyota* sold it through their outlets as the *Glanza*. They both gain. Similarly, look at the tie-up between *Red Hat Enterprise Linux* OS and *Microsoft*. They both compete; however, *Microsoft* offered to host *Red Hat* on their cloud *Azure*. They both gained since *Microsoft* got *Red Hat* customers on their cloud platform.

Partnering with influencers in your industry can increase brand awareness and attract new customers. Look for influencers with a similar target audience to partner with. However, the challenge will be to show such influencers value so they can see mutual benefit in the relationship, or else they may not like to participate.

Businesses can take many special initiatives to increase their revenue and grow. The key is identifying the strategies that align with the customer's needs and drive results.

Sales leaders

A sales leader plays a crucial role in an organisation by ensuring that the sales ecosystem comprising of sales people, technical resources, product development teams, packaging teams and go to market teams all work together to drive the common objective.

Setting sales goals and targets: Define measurable and achievable goals, motivating the sales team to perform at their best. If the organization defines a high sales target, the sales leader should help the team how it will get achieved or else it can become counterproductive.

Developing sales strategies: The sales leader should define the sales strategies that drive revenue growth, increase customer acquisition, and promote customer retention.

For example, looking at the trend the sales leader should decide if they need to go after more customers or increase the value of the deals to drive the organisation's growth. Sales leaders should use these indicators to decide if there is a need to have separate teams for large deals and small deals or if one common team can drive the needed revenue. Similarly, conversion rates reveal lead quality, process effectiveness, and sales team readiness. Regular quarterly analysis and documentation provide insights for reviews and future planning.

Managing the sales budget: The sales leader should manage the sales budget and allocate resources to ensure teams are able to deliver. effectively to achieve the desired sales outcomes. In most developing countries, the sales leaders are not responsible for the budget; hence, they show no interest in reducing costs and increasing business.

The first-line managers

As organisations expand, the first-line managers report to sales leaders and focus on executing tasks in the field. The role of first-line managers is crucial for growth.

First-line managers play a key role in shaping an organisation's culture. They are responsible for setting the tone for employee behaviour, establishing performance standards, and enforcing company policies. Hold them accountable for implementation on the ground.

First-line managers are often employees' first point of contact. They can significantly impact employee engagement and motivation by recognising and rewarding employee achievements, providing regular feedback, and addressing employee concerns.

Define the criteria for making someone a first-line manager, motivating many to work harder to reach that position. For example, one can define that you need a minimum team size of five persons reporting to be called a first-line manager. This will also ensure that the first-line managers put in the needed extra effort to hold on to that position. Overall, it is a win-win for the employee and the organisation.

Need for small value deals team

Multiple factors determine if you need a common sales team to sell high value enterprise solutions and low cost small deals or should you establish different teams. Different teams allow better focus and better conversion. Here are some potential benefits and considerations that can help you decide whether to set up a separate team to manage small deals.

Lower risk: Small deals have a lower risk profile than more significant deals. Second, if things go wrong and you need to refund the money, it will not hurt the organisation's profit and loss (P&L) account.

Faster sales cycle: Since small deals typically have a lower total value, the decision-making can be faster, leading to a shorter sales cycle. This is not necessary, but this is possible with an efficient sales system and some existing product pull in the market. Each Partner Account Managers can work with multiple partners, who in turn work with the end customers. This allow you to manage a bigger territory with less number of sales people.

Limited upside: It is relatively more challenging to secure repeat business from organizations that usually make small purchases as compared to those that engage in large deals. However, some organizations that make small purchases can move to higher-end enterprise deals in due course of time, which is why organisations have small deals team.

Increased competition: Small deals may be more competitive than larger deals, as they may be easier for competitors to replicate or offer similar solutions.

Scalability: Both type of deals have scope of scaling the business. It is the approach which is different, hence organizations should choose the strategy based on their comfort with the type of approach.

The small deal strategy also works as a defensive cum offensive mechanism. When you do multiple small value deals, you help control the competition's reach and get a better product footprint. Gaining entry into a big-value sale can become bit easy.

Enterprise deals team

If you can sell the solution at a higher price by offering more services or a complex solution, consider creating a separate team focusing on such deals. A standard team focussing on all kinds of deals may be an excellent place to start, but it is unsuitable for growing business faster. Particular focus is needed for enterprise deals which has some clear benefits.

Higher revenue: High-value deals can significantly impact the company's revenue and profitability and can often be a key growth driver. The initial few deals can be challenging as teams tend to overcommit when they see a high-value transaction. However, a dedicated and focused team would soon learn how to handle such deals and would be able to manage customer expectations better.

Long-term customers: High-value deals can lead to longer-term customer relationships, providing a stable revenue stream apart from the annuity business, which you can expect from such sales. This also helps innovation as enterprise customers would like to try new innovative things even if that means extra expense. The learnings can be used in similar sales, increasing the organisation's footprint.

Some considerations that can bother any organisation when it gets into high-value sales have been discussed to prepare you better.

Longer sales cycle: High-value deals often have a longer sales cycle, as they typically require more due diligence, negotiation, and approval from multiple stakeholders within the enterprise.

Higher risk: High-value deals have a higher risk of execution than smaller deals, as they may involve a more significant investment of time, resources, and capital from both sides, the customer and the vendor. You will also need more skilled resources to manage customer expectations, as this may need interaction with multiple teams inside the client organisation. At times, one must also work with other external third parties.

Resource intensive: Enterprise deals teams may require more resources and expertise to manage high-value deals effectively. Even for selling high-value deals effectively without leaving loopholes in the contract, one needs more experienced salespeople, and similarly, even for solutions, one needs more experienced technical resources.

Contracting: A separate person or team for contracting enterprise business deals is essential for several reasons. Legal implications can arise during the execution of an enterprise deal, and having a legal expert on the team ensures that the agreement is structured to protect both parties from unforeseen events or issues.

An organisation has to invest in building an enterprise team. Executing a high-value enterprise deal is not just about delivering a product or solution; it is also about managing people and their expectations and maintaining the core team till the execution of the project is over.

Vertical-focused solutions team

A vertical-focused solution is tailored to a specific industry or market segment, such as healthcare, finance, or retail. An organisation can differentiate its product from its competitors by developing solutions that address a particular vertical's unique needs and challenges.

Irrespective of the size of your organisation, positioning a product in a given vertical simplifies the selling job. The basic points one should consider before deciding to get into a vertical focussed sales strategy have been mentioned below.

Subject matter experts: Vertical-focused solutions need subject matter experts who can discuss their understanding of a given industry based on their discussion and implementation of solutions in many other organisations. This knowledge can increase the customer's confidence and help win more deals. Developing such a team with the desired knowledge base takes time and is an ongoing process. This has to be a part of the DNA of the organisation.

Repeatable sales process: Identifying potential customers is easier and the campaigns to help initiate meaningful discussion also becomes simpler.

However, it's important to note that developing vertical-focused solutions can also have some potential drawbacks.

Limited market size: By focusing on a specific vertical, a team may limit its potential market size, which could impact its growth potential. Hence, preferably pick a vertical prevalent in every major geography, and they are there in numbers which will justify the cost of developing such solutions.

Narrow product focus: Focusing on a specific vertical can also limit the team's ability to develop more general-purpose products that could have broader market appeal. Hence, one should look at all possible solutions which can be created for the identified vertical, giving your sales teams more breadth.

Increased complexity: Developing vertical-focused solutions can be more complex and resource-intensive, requiring a deep understanding of a specific industry's unique needs and challenges.

Overall, developing vertical-focused solutions can be a powerful strategy for a team looking to differentiate their product and better align with the needs of their target customers.

The field team and inside-sales team

Inside-sales and field-sales are distinct teams with unique strengths. Field teams delve deep into accounts with intense focus, while inside-sales teams employ a broad, low-touch approach, engaging with significantly more customers. Organisations often combine these teams to target new markets with a shared sales target. Field sales 'go deep and focused', while inside sales 'go wide and shallow'.

Some other differentiating factors have been explained for a better understanding of the value of the different methodologies of going after the market brings to an organisation.

Location: The primary difference between inside-sales and field-sales is where the salespeople conduct their work. Inside-sales teams typically work remotely, using phone, email, and other digital channels to connect with potential customers. In contrast, field sales teams are generally on the field, meeting with customers face-to-face. The inside sales team should be encouraged to travel occasionally to meet customers and partners. When you put a face to the conversation, the trust level goes up, and the understanding of each other improves, making both parties more sensitive to each other's needs.

Cost: Field-sales teams are typically more expensive to operate than inside-sales teams due to travel, lodging, and transportation costs. On the other hand, inside sales teams are more cost-effective because they don't require as much travel.

Reach: Field-sales teams have limited customers who can be reached for physical meetings. There is a limit to the number of potential customers you can physically travel and meet. This is more so if they are geographically dispersed. Much time gets wasted travelling, waiting at the reception, and waiting for your customer to have free time to meet.

Inside-sales teams have the advantage of covering a larger geographic area as they are talking to customers on the phone and by email, making it easier to connect with customers in different regions in a shorter time.

Relationship-building: Field-sales teams have a greater opportunity to build customer relationships, as they can meet face-to-face and establish a personal connection. Inside-sales teams too can build customer relationships but typically rely on digital channels. Hence, many organisations send their inside-sales teams to meet customers and partners. When you put a face to the voice, it becomes more impactful.

Sales process: Field-sales teams are more effective if the decision-making for the product or service you are trying to sell takes time and is slightly expensive. Inside-sales alone may not work in such a sales situation. Building trust is easier in physical meetings. On the other hand, inside-sales teams can often close deals more quickly if the value of what you are selling is lower, and individuals can decide on their own. Usually, such products or solutions have a lower sales cycle.

The field team can comprise two kinds of salespeople. They can be partner account managers, who are expected to work with partners and the direct sales team, who are expected to work with end customers directly. Some organisations prefer not to work with partners at all, and in some cases, they are open to deciding if they would like to work through partners or directly.

Partner account managers and direct sales team

Approaching the market using partner account managers (PAMs) and direct sales teams are two different approaches to sales that businesses can use. They both help you sell and can work in the same market or other markets. Let me explain why you need them and when you will deploy them.

PAMs work with partners to help sell a company's products or services. At the same time, direct sales teams focus on selling products or services directly to customers.

PAMs build relationships with partners and work closely with them to drive sales without meeting the customers on many occasions. Direct sales teams typically build customer relationships and work with customers directly.

PAMs must have strong relationship-building skills and the ability to train and support partners while direct sales teams must have strong sales skills, including prospecting, qualifying leads, and closing sales.

PAMs may be measured based on the performance of their partners, while direct sales teams are often measured based on their individual sales performance.

Organisations use PAMs to open new territories for the organisation. They can also open new market segments in the same market where the organisation is already selling using their direct sales team. Using PAMs to open new territories is a low-cost, practical approach to opening a new market.

The choice between PAMs or direct sales teams will depend on the business's specific sales goals and strategy. PAMs can be a good option for companies looking to scale their sales efforts through partnerships. In contrast, direct sales teams can be a good option for businesses looking to sell directly to customers.

Some businesses may use both approaches simultaneously to maximise their sales efforts. In such an approach, the direct salesperson can sell directly to the end customer or can sell to customers through a partner. His job is to maximise sales irrespective of the route to market. The PAM's performance will be measured based on his partners' performance, and any deal done directly with the customer without any involvement from the partner will not be considered a PAM deal.

Training team

Sales training can help your team members develop their skills and knowledge, leading to improved sales performance. Training can help them understand the sales process, how to prospect and qualify leads, how to negotiate effectively, and how to close deals. Once your team is ready, you must do the same for your ecosystem partners.

Rolling out capsuled programs for internal teams, partners, and customers can be an effective way to help them better understand product usage. The best way to deliver the program can include online modules, webinars, in-person workshops, or a combination of these methods.

A well-trained team is better equipped to provide excellent customer service. They can answer questions more effectively, address concerns and objections, and provide customers with the information to make informed purchasing decisions.

More than 90% of Indian organisations do not run regular, meaningful training sessions, and hence, lack of knowledge becomes a big bottleneck and forces organisations not to grow beyond a point.

BPOT teams and territories

The difference between these two methods is who sells the company's products or services within a territory. In a Business Partner Owned Territory or BPOT model, the partner is responsible for the entire sales process, working with a channel sales resource aligned to that territory who will meet face-to-face with customers and partners. However, selling cannot be done without the involvement of a partner.

In a BPOT territory, the channel team and its partner's network are entirely responsible for the sales process, from lead generation to closing the sale. Partners usually work on commission, which they earn on their sales.

The BPOT model can help companies expand their reach into new markets and increase sales without always adding to their internal sales team. However, this model also requires a strong partnership with the ecosystem in that geography.

Therefore, organisations create a small team, which is usually part of the channel sales team and can pick multiple territories where the organisation would like to expand without spending too much money. This team is the BPOT team, which leverages the partner ecosystem to drive revenue. Dedicated field-sales, if any, are known as the Partner Account Managers.

A BPOT model can be a cost-effective way for an organisation to enter a new market or expand its sales reach without having to incur the expenses of building and maintaining an in-house sales team. Using a BPOT model, the organisation can also benefit from the partner's existing sales network, which can help them reach a broader range of potential customers without building their network from scratch. This can save the organisation time and resources and help them achieve faster results. Hence, a BPOT model can be an effective strategy for organisations looking to enter a new market or expand their sales reach with limited resources or expertise in the local market.

If an organisation from India wants to enter the Brazilian market to do business, it can assign one channel sales person to that geography. He can then sign up with a local partner, preferably a distributor kind of person if there is some pull for the existing product or solution. If the product or the service is entirely unknown and you do not have a reasonable budget for marketing, consider signing up with a partner who has the potential to grow and can work as your organisation's extended arm.

This one person (channel salesperson) from the principal will create an ecosystem of partners, generate leads, and drive some business. This model helps you start your work at a much lower expense, and you can even learn the legal and sales nuances of the market. Once business picks up and justifies setting up your local team, you can think of opening up a branch office or deploying your own sales team without calling it a branch office.

Once you call that small setup your branch office, visibility goes up, and the responsibility of fulfilling the legal compliance issues in a foreign land also gets added. This can only be done once you understand the basics and are ready to plunge. You can try this model in five different countries simultaneously by aligning only sales resources for each country, and after two to three years, you can decide which two countries you want to focus more on.

Academic initiative team

Working with academia can be a great way to improve the reach and increase the visibility and presence of your products and services. You can partner with universities and introduce your company to students who may become potential future customers or employees. You need to explain to the academia the benefit they will get by partnering with you and how you can help the students and the teaching staff.

Partnering with academia to collaborate on research projects can not only help advance your own research and development efforts but can also help increase the visibility of your company's work to a broader audience.

Consider offering guest lectures or workshops at universities to help them better integrate with the industry and not just your organisation. You can use this opportunity to showcase your products and services to students. Help them learn how to use the product based on different-uses cases. This can help build brand recognition and create interest among students apart from assisting them in learning something which can help them in their job prospects.

You can sponsor student competitions or events, help raise your company's profile among the student community, and potentially attract future customers or employees. *IBM* used to organise 'The Great Mind Challenge', where students were asked to create solutions using tools that are generic as well as related to *IBM*. Some 1,400 colleges from 29 states and union territories participated in this coding cum solution preparing competition. Students learnt programming, working in a team, designing, and developing solutions which people need. This made them industry-ready. This helped *IBM* as well as the academia. One can do the same with their product line. Not everyone will become your customer later, but some will.

Look for something other than commercial benefits in the first year. You are now running a marathon, so have patience, and you will be able to see the results.

Knowledge management team

Knowledge management refers to creating, sharing, using, and managing knowledge and information within an organisation. Create a portal and popularise it. This can help organisations in several ways, including:

Improved decision-making: Knowledge management can help organisations make better decisions by providing access to relevant and reliable information.

Increased innovation: By sharing knowledge and encouraging collaboration, organisations can foster a culture of innovation and creativity. Easy access will also increase productivity.

Better customer service: Organisations can quickly address customer inquiries and concerns with a centralised knowledge base. It can do this by creating a customer forum in the portal by uploading the frequently asked questions and answers or by helping them learn about other customers using your product and solution.

Increased competitiveness: Knowledge management can help organisations stay competitive by leveraging their knowledge and expertise to develop new products and services, improve processes, and stay ahead of industry trends. Many customers can contribute to the site by sharing their unique experiences, if any, which can then be incorporated into the next version of your product or solution.

Increase usage of the knowledge base: Ask for contributions from users for a fee. Organise meetings and conferences of the authors or existing contributors.

Chase the number of users on the site: Every year, find ways to increase the number of visitors to your site. Monitor it monthly. Look for new and unique visitors. One should run different kinds of digital campaigns to help reach out to more potential visitors and give them a good reason to visit your site.

Coffee table discussion: Hire a few seats in a popular coffee shop at a time when fewer customers visit the coffee shop. Invite your select guests to discuss topics of interest, including technology, deployment of solutions, new ideas, and new ways of using the product or solution. This approach helps increase customer relationships and helps cultivate a more loyal customer base.

Google encourages innovation and experimentation by giving employees time and resources to work on passion projects. This allows employees to explore new ideas and technologies that may not directly relate to their job responsibilities.

IBM developerWorks is an online resource and community for software developers and IT professionals. It is a platform for sharing knowledge, collaborating on projects, and finding resources to help developers improve their skills and stay up-to-date with emerging technologies.

Centre of excellence team

A centre of excellence or CoE team specialises in a particular area or function and provides leadership, best practices, research, support, and training to other organisational departments or groups. The main goal of a CoE is to promote and maintain excellence in a specific area, such as technology, operations, finance, or customer service. It is typically made up of experts with deep knowledge and experience in the field who work together to develop and implement best practices, standards, and processes that can be shared with other departments.

Many software companies have a CoE for banking, insurance, shared services, or government practice, depending on the area they want to specialise in and compete. They work with customers of that vertical across different geographies; hence, they bring much value, which, often, even the customer may have yet to see.

When I managed the *Linux Software* business for *IBM* in 2005, a four-person CoE team was aligned with me to help the sales and technical teams inside the organisation by checking out potential high-value solutions in the lab. The experimentation in the lab ensured that the solution you suggested to your customer would work. The team also conducted training sessions for some customers across the country. This helped encourage many sales teams to approach the CoE for help, and they took the solutions to their customers without any fear of getting into technical issues.

In terms of selling, having a CoE can help organisations differentiate themselves from their competitors by showcasing their expertise and knowledge in a particular area. This can help build customer trust and credibility, increasing sales and revenue. Additionally, a CoE can provide a platform for organisations to develop and showcase innovative solutions and services, which can also help to attract and retain customers.

Customer experience centre

A customer experience centre is usually a centralised location or platform where businesses can interact and engage with their customers to provide a positive experience.

In my *IBM* days, I saw one such centre. It was a nice place to bring your customers where standard solution demonstrations were running. You can take your solution expert there and then organise a meeting with the potential customer. It helps build a positive feeling and encourages the customer to make a favourable decision. At *SCO*, when selling the Unix operating system, we had a demo centre, which could double up as a customer experience centre. It was part of the office. A separate prominent cubicle place.

Many customers were curious to know how failover worked and what happened if a person tried to get his boarding pass at the airport and the power failed. Would the system issue two boarding passes for the same seat? Could it save what was on the screen during a power failure? How would the backup server start working, and how long it would take? The demo centre could showcase this in front of the customer. It was impressive, and it helped in selling.

So, pick the most impressive part of your product or solution and showcase it to the customers along with the storyline to help them understand the value. They can then relate the same to their business and decide.

One can even create a virtual customer experience centre, where the goal is to create a seamless and consistent experience across all customer touchpoints, such as online, in-store, and via phone or email. The centre may provide a range of services to customers, such as product or service information, technical support, customer service, and feedback gathering.

Customer experience centres may be physical locations, such as a dedicated physical space retail store, or virtual platforms like a website or mobile application. Technology, such as artificial intelligence and chatbots, can also help to automate and enhance the customer experience.

Overall, the customer experience centre is essential in building customer loyalty, driving sales, and improving brand reputation by providing personalised and high-quality customer service.

Retain the team

Retaining 90% of the team is as good as working on a new strategy. The sheer fact that the team continues will mean additional business. An existing team will better understand the company culture, processes, and procedures. This can help them be more efficient and effective in their work. An existing team also has already established relationships and dynamics, which can make it easier to work together and communicate effectively. Finally, an existing team has likely worked with the company's products or services for a while, giving them a deeper understanding of what the company does and how to serve customers best.

Some attrition is good, so let that happen, but avoid having a situation of mass exodus. A new hire brings a fresh perspective and new ideas, which can help the team innovate and improve. A new hire may also have skills or expertise that the existing team doesn't have, which can help fill a skills gap and enhance the team's overall capabilities.

Ultimately, what you need is the right mixture. Some infusion of new blood regularly will do good, but too many of them compared to the existing team may mean chaos, a lot of extra training effort, and still need to catch up.

The key here is to choose the right components, finetune the functioning of the teams, and strategise the processes in such a way that your organisation works like a war machine. This will give your sales department much-needed confidence.

12
CHAPTER

Building the Strategy

A sales strategy is a plan of action designed to achieve specific sales objectives, such as increasing revenue, acquiring new customers, or penetrating a new market.

A well-designed sales strategy should consider the target market, competition, pricing, and marketing initiatives, among other factors, to create a comprehensive plan that aligns with the overall business goals. By following a sales strategy, sales teams can work more efficiently, identify new opportunities, and build stronger customer relationships, leading to increased sales and business growth.

Strategy is the overall plan for achieving a goal. A successful outcome often requires a well-designed strategy supported by effective tactics.

Tactics and strategy are often interchangeably used, but they are fundamentally different. The golden rule is that strategy remains constant while the tactics can keep changing based on ground realities. Tactics mean the specific actions taken to implement the strategy. They are the steps or methods used to execute the plan and achieve the desired outcome.

Many small and mid-sized companies do not value 'strategy' much. It is considered as a fancy thing. So, the organisation does not proceed based on any comprehensive plan to address the market.

In 2001, when I worked with *SCO* selling the *Unix* operating system or with *IBM* promoting the *IBM* stack on *Linux*, I met many small and mid-sized IT companies to explore the potential of leveraging their reach and network to work with them jointly.

Most started the financial year without really having laid down any strategy. It was all in the head of the owner of the business. In most cases, they never had a defined market segment they wanted to work with, nor did they had any defined way of approaching potential customers. Sales were completely dependent on the individual brilliance of the salesperson.

I have witnessed a similar thing in the global market, too. Their strategy was not to have any strategy. No wonder many of these organisations never grow beyond a point. Many shut down their business after a few years as they cannot add new customers, and the revenue from old customers does not justify the business.

An effective strategy can give you the differentiating factor and even improve your business execution. What *Indigo Airlines* did by providing the ramp to help customers get up and down quickly, holding their luggage or taking a wheelchair, has given them an edge in positioning themselves better as a friendly airline. It has helped them cut down the time needed for passengers to get up and get down from the aircraft. Consequently, they were landing and taking off in time, positioning them as professional airlines. That did help them do more business with everything else remaining constant. That is what a strategy does to your business.

A well-defined strategy typically includes several key components:

Vision and Mission: Define the organisation's vision in simple words that everyone can understand and appreciate. This is usually for the overall organisation.

Goals and Objectives: This can be for the organisation or the department. Define the goals you want to achieve and which will lead to achieving the vision. Goals should be clearly defined and achievable, so define the timeline for achieving the objective. The goal can be to reach a turnover of 100 crores in two years or achieve a 15% market share in your segment in two countries.

Analysis and Assessment: Do a SWOT analysis. Analyse the current status and where you want to be and define the parameters to assess if you are growing in the right direction and at the right pace.

Strategic Choices: Define the market you want to enter and the segment you would like to enter. Define the strategy for the same. This can mean if you wish to sell directly or through partners. Do you want to start by introducing low-cost products first or expensive products first or all of them?

Resource Allocation: Define the resources you will need to achieve the objective and your hiring and induction plan to make things happen. Give due timelines, including provision for training and onboarding of new or existing staff from different departments. All resource induction should be aligned with the strategic objective of the organisation.

Implementation Plan: This is the complex part. Look at the departments and people who will be involved at different levels and timeframe for different activities to be initiated and monitored. Involve the stakeholders and take their feedback to incorporate them into the plan.

Risk Management: Every strategy will have a risk factor. Make provision for it and plan accordingly to minimise the risks. For example, if there is a dispute with the customer, would you like to go to court or refund the money and settle? Do you want to insure the business to cover the risks, or do you think it may not be needed in the initial phase? You may like to write down, discuss and decide on many such issues.

Continuous Evaluation and Adaptation: Any strategy must be monitored regularly to see the impact on the ground and make changes if needed. Hence, continuous evaluation and course correction at regular intervals should be part of the strategy.

Overall, strategy provides a roadmap for guiding decision-making and resource allocation, aligning organisational efforts, and achieving long-term goals in a competitive and dynamic business environment.

There are few things which are important in any strategy session as they will have an impact on the people and the business. Some of them have been listed for easy understanding.

Identify the universe

Also known as the addressable market, identifying the addressable market or universe where a sales team should operate and sell is mandatory for any business, as it helps to focus the team's efforts and resources on the most promising opportunities. However, most small and mid-sized companies do not define the universe. They have a vague definition at the most. Even vertical definition is uncommon; hence, they spread themselves too thin, get too little business done, and blame everyone else except their selling strategy. Here are some steps to identify the addressable market:

Define your ideal customer: Consider the characteristics of your ideal customer, such as industry, company size, location, budget, and pain points, which should help you narrow down the universe of potential customers.

Analyse the market: Use market research reports to analyse your target market's size and growth potential, as well as the competitive landscape and trends in the industry.

Market segmentation: Divide your target market into segments based on industry, vertical, and capacity to pay. The effective division will help you tailor your sales and marketing efforts to each part. You should build a database of customers based on these criteria and stick to the universe for all your business development activities in any given financial year.

Frequently changing the universe is not good for business. However, when under pressure, the sales team will always keep changing the universe, hoping they might get a deal from those accounts they previously thought were not good enough. In the bargain, they never manage to develop the addressable market to a point where getting business at regular intervals can become a reality.

So, one can ask, what is the need for defining the universe? Organisations define the universe for the sales team for multiple reasons. One important reason is to focus on the market and benefit from your work in that market even later. Priming the customer can take time; however, your sales team may not be there to sell when the customer is ready to buy. They would have given up on them and focused on some other customer. Your competition would have gone and made the sale.

It is vital to put blinkers on the eyes of the horses on the race course during a race so that they don't lose focus, and don't get terrified by the huge crowd or the competing horses in the race track. Similarly, defining the universe and making the sales team focus and work in that market segment for better results is equally important. Have a separate group if needed, to focus on the other undefined market. Put a system in place to manage known accounts and unknown accounts. Even the unknown accounts should not be infinite.

Now, the follow-up question can be, how does defining a universe help in the long run? Once the universe is specified, every sales, marketing, or lead generation team can focus on that list. There is no need to search for customer databases separately by different groups to run their respective campaigns. Second, when potential customers keep hearing about the company and their products and solutions regularly, some may become customers in the first year, and some in the second or third year. This becomes possible because the customer learns about the new products and solutions through various marketing campaigns year after year. Hence, his chances of getting converted as a customer becomes high.

The next question that many may have is, why should organisations define the universe for each salesperson? Is it necessary? Yes, it is necessary. It reduces internal conflicts as everyone will know which customer is being managed by whom; hence, even if someone tries to work on an account and close a deal quietly, the sale will get registered only in that person's name, in whose universe the customer was present. This ensures almost zero conflict based on accounts.

Second, it reduces injustice to the new person in the team. Usually, when you do not have a system, the good accounts where business is assured are picked up by the favourite of the big boss. The rest of the team struggles. This unfair distribution of territory or accounts leads to poor work culture and results. The system can largely control such bias and can help the business grow.

Escop has been an IT firm in the business for the last ten years. They do define a universe but never follow it sincerely. Let us understand how it can impact the business.

Sales leader: Rajesh, I have not seen any business from you for six months. If things continue like this, you can get into trouble. What are you doing to get some business?

Rajesh (Salesperson): I will change the potential customer list. I've selected some organisations that are reasonably big and did have the potential to buy. Unfortunately, no business came from there. I will add a new customer list and drop some earlier ones.

Sales leader: Good. It is better late than never.

After three months of this conversation, news arrives that M/s Kamra, a client organisation, finally bought the solution at a reasonable price. The sales leader and Rajesh rush to M/s Kamra's office to discuss.

Sales leader: Sir (CIO), I assumed you would send us the proposal request before deciding on the solution. We did a proof of concept (POC) for your organisation last year, which your team liked.

CIO: Yes, you are correct that your organisation did a POC, and we not only liked it, but we also learned a few things from it. You are right in saying that we should have invited you. Unfortunately, when you went out of sight, you also went out of mind. Some new team members did not know about your organisation and did not invite you. Sorry for that. However, we have already taken a decision that cannot be reversed. Maybe next time.

It was sad that after doing all the groundwork, educating the customer, and creating the needed environment inside the organisation to help them decide to buy the solution, the sales team was not there to make the sale happen and benefit from that. Things like this happen quite regularly when you do not follow the concept of defining the universe and nurturing the defined universe of customers.

Think global and act local

The benefits of global standardisation need to be balanced with the need for local adaptation. Although businesses operate in a globalised world with interconnected markets and shared trends, they must also tailor their strategies and operations to suit the unique characteristics and preferences of local markets.

The concept of thinking globally involves understanding the global marketplace in a broader context. The identification of overarching trends, taking advantage of opportunities, the challenges businesses face across borders.

It involves developing a cohesive global strategy that aligns with the overarching goals and values of the organisation, leveraging economies of scale, standardising processes, and sharing best practices across different markets. Thinking globally enables businesses to capitalize on global opportunities, maintain consistency in branding and messaging, and achieve synergies across regions. So the strategy remains constant however based on the geography the tactics can change.

So if the strategy is to go for large customers and large deals, the strategy will remain constant across geographies or if the strategy is that a Small Deals team will work on smaller value deals in the next step of defined accounts, then the same strategy will work in all geographies however the way of approaching the market and convincing the customers can differ.

Developing a sales play for different geographies and market segments can help a business tailor its approach to each unique market and maximise its potential for success. Provides a brief overview of the key features and benefits of the product, the target customer persona, and the typical pain points that the product is designed to address. Include a list of questions a salesperson should ask to uncover the customer's needs and objections and a suggested script to help answer those queries as a starting point of the conversation.

Localise the brochure and the video to help customers understand what you are trying to sell.

Integration with third-party tools to sell more: Integrating with a third-party tool at global level can help you take the solution to all geographies where a market exists, however one should identify local strong players, integrating with whom can make your offerings strong in that local market. This mutually beneficial relationship should help in the respective local markets.

This way, integrating with a third-party tool can create a win-win situation for both organisations. However, that does not mean a more prominent OEM (original equipment manufacturer) like *Microsoft* or *IBM*, who have hundreds of such partners, will give you priority and do the selling for you. Their salespeople will help customers understand that different solutions exist on their platform, may even name a few, and then leave it to the buyer to decide. They will sell what sells quickly; hence, run marketing activities and create pull for your products and services.

Identify partners in those geographies: You can have tie up with some global partners or customers who can help you do business in a new geography, however you will also need to identify partners who serve or have presence in the respective local market.

Brand reputation: When you are new in a geography, use reference of other markets to establish trust. In some cases, your international wins and global tie ups can help establish a better rapport than your local customer base or local tie ups. So explore options and decide on the strategy which will help you win.

Creating the partner network

If you are selling a known product, it is not difficult. However, the job becomes difficult if you sell a product that people in that country do not know about. More so, if it is a well-served country where people are already used to multiple options, introducing a new product is always a herculean task. Spending marketing dollars is a must, or the right type of partners may not sign up.

The salesperson would like to sell what can be sold quickly. Selling an unknown product or solution is always tricky, so salespeople avoid it. Sometimes, the partner will sign up but stop working after a few months when they do not see sales happening. However, if you can show deals are happening, partners will continue putting in the effort.

How many partners you should have in any geography will depend on your presence there. If you are new, you cannot be choosy; hence, you may sign up with more than one partner, get some market access, do some groundwork, and then stick to one or two partners, as the case may be. However, the addressable market for the product or solution should help define the number of partners one can sign up for. A mass-selling product can have hundreds of partners in a country.

Many of your partners won't help you get business. You'll likely get business from around 20% of your partner network, but managing multiple partners can be challenging. It is difficult to determine which partners will contribute to the project and which won't, so having a larger network is helpful.

Remember, when partners sign up, they believe they can do business together. The partner invests in people and spends money on travel and other expenses to do business. Similarly, even the product company spend money on training and lead generation campaigns and helps the partner run with opportunities where sales can happen. Unfortunately, it does not always work. Unlike in maths or physics, sales results cannot be known and predicted, hence the need to take the risk.

You must treat your partners or dealers as an extended arm, just like you treat your own sales team. The way you need to run with your sales team, support them, guide them, and motivate them to deliver results. It would help if you did the same with your partner; otherwise, results may not arrive.

The only difference between the partner's team and your team is the salary component. The partner resources work for you without getting paid, so you need to be more considerate, patient, and forthcoming in helping them do business, or else you may lose them.

Organisations try to create an ecosystem of business partners and then get upset when they do not see results. The above clarifications should help organisations understand how to engage with their partner ecosystem.

Prioritise the markets
Prioritise the markets based on their potential for growth and profitability. Consider factors such as market size, competition, your organisation's capability to sell in that market and customer demand for your product.

Allocate resources based on the potential of each market. This may include sales personnel, marketing budgets, and other resources needed to penetrate each market effectively. Measure your sales' effectiveness in each geography and market segment, and adjust your approach as needed. This may involve refining your tactics, reallocating resources, or entering or exiting specific markets.

By following these steps, a business can identify different geographies and market segments and develop a customised approach that maximises its potential for success in each market. Remember that a low-budget entry into a new market will demand patience and hard work. Don't shy away from that. Allocate a marketing budget and participate in industry events.

Well-served market and under-served market

You need to have two kinds of approach. One for the well-served market and the other one for the under-served market. The USA or Western Europe is a well-served market. They had the advantage of working with global giants in their respective fields. They are used to working with the established players. Hence, unknown organisations will struggle to get an audience with the right kind of potential customers or business partners.

However, the geography where not many global giants go and sell directly can be categorised as under-served markets, where they may not have the exposure or understanding of the best possible products and solutions. In some cases, even if they have the exposure, they may find it difficult to get good quality support on that product or solution line. So, the option to choose from many is limited and sometimes very limited. So, a new company may find selling in the under-served market easier.

Entering a well-served market is like swimming with sharks. You need experienced and seasoned team members to work on a strategy and on the execution of that strategy to reap benefits. Start by participating in local exhibitions. Put up a professional show so that people take an interest in walking into your stall and talking to you. A regular booth will not attract the crowd; people will look at you from a distance and walk away. So, make things interesting. Make it glamorous. Glamour sells everywhere in the world. This is the first step.

Second, highlight those aspects of your product which will differentiate you from the leaders. Selling products is much more challenging than selling services in most well-served markets, as they usually lack enough skilled resources. So, work on the packaging and presentation of the product. Packaging means documentation, video, etc. to help customers use your product.

Organise webinars and try to get a local speaker. Find ways to attract partners to sign up with you. Finding good partners anywhere in the world is complex; getting a partner who will agree to represent an unknown brand is difficult in a well-served market. So don't be too choosy in the initial phase. You should know, that just because you have signed up with some big, capable partners, does not mean they will go and start selling for you. They will sell what is acceptable to the customers in the market and sell quickly. So, you still need to go out, meet customers, and create the required pull.

In most cases, the established partners may not run with you from the beginning. They will meet you halfway. You may never get to see them if we do not reach that mid-point. Their logic is simple. They were not incorporated to help you grow; they are there to develop their organisation and hence, will work with those who they think will help them grow. Promoting a new product or solution needs much work which needs to be done by the product manufacturer. Partners will only assist those products which are visible in the addressable market.

Getting listed in the marketplace is not enough

Getting listed in marketplaces like *Amazon* and *Flipkart* is just the beginning. You have to work on a go-to-market plan for each of them. Ultimately, success will depend on reaching the end customers and talking to them about your product. Execution of the strategy is the key here, and it will depend on the effort you put into making it happen.

Meeting more relevant end customers and helping them understand what you have has to be constantly done by you in significant numbers. This will make you visible, and this will help you push the ecosystem to run with you and help you sell.

You should know that it is worth the effort. One can do much more business in a well-served market than what you do in an under-served market. However, the challenge is doing multiple activities and leveraging all possible help from different teams in your home country to make things happen. A small team working in a silo will struggle to succeed in this competitive market. So, find your niche, show value, and use the full ecosystem to reach the customer segment. You will be happy that you did all this.

The director of a product distribution company in Sydney once told me something many may find strange. He said, 'I came out of my room to meet you in person as you are the first person from India who has bothered to fly down to our country and meet us in our office. Usually, we get phone calls and emails. Too many of them. So, my suggestion is that you enter the market if you are ready to spend more than the payroll expenses of your staff.'

Webinars and seminars for visibility

Webinars and seminars can be tools for gaining visibility and priming the market. Hosting a these can showcase your expertise and knowledge to a targeted audience. They can help build your reputation and establish you as a thought leader in your industry.

Webinars and seminars also provide a platform to interact with potential customers, answer their questions directly, and help build trust and credibility, ultimately leading to increased sales. In addition, they help generate leads and grow your email list. By asking attendees to register for the event, you can capture their contact information and follow up with them afterwards to nurture the relationship.

Joint go-to-market with your partners

Joint GTM (go-to-market) is a business strategy where two or more companies collaborate to promote and sell their products or services to a common target market. This strategy enables companies to pool resources and leverage their strengths to achieve common business objectives.

Most organisations do create a GTM to sell what they have. However, many do not understand how to create a plan while working with business partners. Here are some steps that can help in developing a joint GTM strategy with partners:

Define the objectives: The first step in a joint GTM strategy is identifying the partnership's objectives. The partners should agree on what they want to achieve, what products or services they wish to sell, and the target market they want to reach.

Assess partner capabilities: Evaluating each partner's strengths, weaknesses, and capabilities is essential in helping identify how each partner can contribute to the partnership. If the partner is a global giant, then using their name and logo can help get visibility. On the other hand, if the partner is small but active and present locally, they can help reach out to more customers.

Develop a joint value proposition: The partners should work together to create a joint value proposition that clearly articulates the benefits of the partnership. A clear and concise messaging strategy should communicate this value proposition to the target market and how it will help the end customer. All the extra benefits they get should be highlighted.

Agree on roles and responsibilities: In any GTM, multiple activities must be done to make the campaign successful. Depending on the strength of the organisations, they should decide on the role they can play in making the campaign a success.

Create a joint marketing plan: Create a marketing plan that outlines the marketing activities, timelines, and budget for the joint GTM strategy. Many organisations create a standard template for this and fill the needed part, as the activities can differ from campaign to campaign or market to market.

Establish metrics for success: The partners should establish metrics to measure the success of the joint GTM strategy. This can include revenue targets, customer acquisition, customer satisfaction, and other key performance indicators.

Monitor and evaluate: Finally, the partners should monitor and evaluate the success of the joint GTM strategy. This will help identify areas of improvement and adjust the strategy as needed.

A joint GTM strategy can be a powerful way to leverage the strengths of multiple partners to achieve common business objectives. By following these steps, partners can develop a successful joint GTM strategy that delivers value to their customers and drives business growth.

Lead generation

Lead generation is crucial in driving sales for any business. Hire smart people who understand business and treat them like your backend sales team. Whether you should do lead generation on your own or hire a third party, as there are multiple organisations specialising in lead generation that have come up, one needs to evaluate the options before deciding the way out.

With an in-house team, you have more control over the quality of work, the processes, and the tools used for lead generation. Your in-house team will likely be more familiar with your product or service and the nuances of your target market. This can help them create more effective messaging and strategies for lead generation.

However, the biggest disadvantage of having your own team for lead generation is cost. Hiring and training an in-house team can be expensive, especially if you need to invest in additional tools or technology like CRM tools, a database of customers, team managers, etc.

An external service provider can scale up or down quickly based on your needs without additional hiring or training. This is a big plus. Sometimes, outsourcing lead generation can be more cost-effective than hiring and training an in-house team. You also do not have to invest space to allow the team to operate outside your office.

The drawbacks associated with external service provider is that you have less control over the quality of work and the processes used for lead generation. When working with an external service provider, communication can be challenging, especially if they speak a different language. Many a time, companies trying to operate in a different country or geography hire agencies who speak the local language. The team hired for this service will only be able to communicate well when they learn about the product and solution properly, which in itself can be a challenge.

Lead progression campaigns

Lead progression campaigns are a series of marketing activities designed to nurture potential leads and give them the extra push they need to make the sales happen.

Define customer journey: The first step in developing a lead progression campaign is to define the customer's journey and understand the potential reason for the delay in decision-making. By analysing the customer journey, you can create campaigns tailored to each stage of the process.

Develop targeted content: Once you have identified the different stages of the customer journey, you can create targeted content that addresses the needs and concerns of potential customers at each stage. This can include blog posts, whitepapers, case studies, videos, and other types of content.

Marketing automation: Marketing automation tools can create personalised campaigns triggered based on customer behaviour, such as website visits, form submissions, and email opens. These tools can deliver targeted content to potential customers.

Leverage email marketing: Email marketing is key to leading progression campaigns. Sending targeted emails to potential customers addressing their potential concerns can be a game changer. Analyse them and take the next steps accordingly.

Lead progression campaigns can effectively nurture potential leads and move them closer to purchasing. Creating a landing page is one important thing which organisations can do to help their customers make a favourable decision.

Landing Page: Creating a landing page specifically for a target market is a great way to interact with the audience and drive sales. By focusing on the products or solutions most relevant to that region, you can create a more personalised experience for potential customers, increasing their interest and engagement.

To create an effective landing page:

i) Keep the messaging clear and focused,

ii) Highlight the key benefits of your products or solutions and provide compelling calls to action,

iii) Use good-quality images and videos to make the page visually appealing,

iv) Have a call to action to ensure interested customers know what to do next.

To drive traffic to your landing page, you can use search engines like *Google* to target relevant keywords and increase visibility. You can also use social media and other online advertising platforms to reach your target audience and direct them to your landing page. Finally, it's important to measure the impact of your landing page by tracking traffic growth and conversion rates.

Hygiene factors

In sales, hygiene factors refer to the basic requirements for effective sales performance.

a. Dress up for the occasion: People will judge you based on how you dress up. Your clothing and appearance can send signals to others about your personality, professionalism, and even your level of success. How you dress will create the first impression in the customer's mind. People may make assumptions or judgments based on your appearance.

In May 2005, I received a call saying that I needed to reach the Chandigarh Secretariat the next day for a meeting with some senior government people. I had joined *IBM* a month earlier, I was new to the system and did not know much about the basic unwritten rules. I was asked to carry my suit.

I checked into a hotel from where around 12 of us went for the meeting at 10am at the secretariat. Everyone was supposed to talk about their specialisation and not try to hog the limelight. When ten of us walked into the secretariat wearing suits and a laptop bag on our shoulders, I could feel the commotion in the office of the senior government official. Frantic calls were being made to have an equal number of representatives from the government side, too. One thing was obvious—we had created the needed impact. I had never seen such an impact of a visiting sales team on any organisation. Irrespective of what you sell, dressing up for the occasion is essential.

b. Return mail after every call: Creating business meeting minutes and sending them to everyone concerned should be strictly followed to ensure everyone is on the same page. The minutes can act as a reference point later.

In addition, sending the minutes of meeting can also serve as documentation. If there are any disputes or questions in the future, the minutes can be referred to as a record of what was discussed and agreed upon during the meeting. Overall, it is a good practice that can help ensure effective communication and collaboration among team members.

c. Do not defend the indefensible: When faced with a mistake or an issue that cannot be defended, trying to argue or debate the issue can often worsen the situation. It can create an adversarial atmosphere and damage relationships, both with colleagues and clients or customers.

Instead, accepting responsibility for the mistake and showing a willingness to make things right can help ease tensions and create a positive impression. It shows you are mature, responsible, and committed to finding a solution. Additionally, an honest and accountable person is liked and appreciated by most.

d. It is okay to lose a deal occasionally: In sales, some deals will inevitably be lost. Do not get discouraged. Use the experience as a learning opportunity. By analysing, salespeople can improve their approach and increase their chances of success in future deals.

Besides, it is crucial to maintain a positive attitude and not take rejection personally. Salespeople should remember that a lost deal does not reflect their professional value or worth. By staying positive and focusing on learning and improvement, salespeople can maintain their motivation and confidence, even in the face of rejection. This can help them stay focused on their goals and pursue new opportunities with enthusiasm and determination.

e. Acknowledge help from others: Acknowledging the contribution of colleagues from the same team or other teams helps to build mutual trust and respect. When valued and appreciated, team members are more likely to feel motivated and engaged in their work. This can lead to increased productivity, better collaboration, and better overall business outcomes. In addition, it can help build strong relationships between team members, leading to more effective collaboration and teamwork.

Hygiene factors in sales are essential for building trust, credibility, and strong relationships with potential customers. Salespeople who prioritise these factors can create a positive reputation for themselves and their company, leading to long-term sales success.

What is the challenge in creating a strategy?
The challenge is that an approach is often made based on the top management's gut feelings, not ground reality. So, if the top management decides that instead of 15% growth, which a company is growing at traditionally, they will grow at the rate of 50% for the next two years, that becomes the plan, and everybody starts working on the strategy to achieve that growth without understanding how they will make it happen. This makes target achievement difficult, if not impossible.

Organisations should check why we think 50% growth is possible and not 100%. Why could we not do it earlier? What will happen if we do not grow at this pace? Will it impact the organisation financially? What new actions are we planning to do to achieve that growth? We need to ask ourselves what has changed so we can suddenly grow at that pace. How robust are the assumptions? Market conditions are changing rapidly, and so is the landscape of competition. Are you taking necessary precautions to ensure the new ground rules do not disrupt your plan?

In 1987, when I entered the IT industry, *dBASE III Plus* was the market leader in the database business. It took a few years before it released *dBASE IV*. The same was true for *Lotus 123*, the market leader in spreadsheet business, and *Wordstar*, the market leader in word-processing business. However, nowadays, a new version comes up every six months, and every year, more than one new competing organisation joins the bandwagon, offering more features. So, everything is changing quickly, and your assumptions based on last year's performance may not be valid because of all these changes in the marketplace.

Hence, do not just assume things without thinking hard. *Wordstar* was the global market leader for many years, and then *WordPerfect* changed everything. Overnight, the leadership of *Wordstar* was gone. They could not revive after that. The market leader vanished from the market. So, avoid projecting next year's business based on the past year without due diligence. Similarly, for many years, *dBASE III Plus* and *Foxbase+* dominated the database market globally. Then came the concept of RDBMS (Relational Database Management) software. Soon, everyone was talking about these new products, and *dBASE III Plus* and *Foxbase+* vanished from the marketplace. So, keep questioning your plan, be open to ideas and suggestions, and be open to critical feedback. The challenge is that we do not question the target or the strategy and spend much money achieving an unrealistic plan. This is one reason many organisations get disappointed when they do not achieve their goals.

13
CHAPTER

Make Some Noise and Become Visible

The first step to selling a product or service is getting potential customers to know that an organisation exists. They should also know how to get in touch with the organisation or with the partner of the organisation in their respective geography to ask for the product or service. To do that, the organisation concerned should have the product and make noise about it. The more noise you make, the more visible you become, and your chances of making the sales happen also increase.

Marketing should explore the various options for taking their message to the customer. Even educating customers to understand the value and purpose of buying a solution is also part of marketing. So, divide your expense budget into multiple buckets.

It can be spending money to promote the ecosystem, educating the potential audience, and organising workshops, seminars, or roadshows to gain visibility. There are many options and things to do, as building the right ecosystem and priming the market takes time, effort, and money.

In marketing, one can use traditional or Digital media depending on customers' demographics. Interestingly, the established traditional media of print and television is under attack from global giants like *Google*, *Facebook*, *Instagram*, *Amazon*, and others. Traditional media still accounts for a significant percentage of advertising, but digital advertising is rapidly gaining importance and is expected to continue to grow.

Digital advertising offers several advantages over traditional media, including targeting specific audiences based on demographics, interests, and behaviour. It also allows for real-time tracking and analysis of ad performance, enabling businesses to make data-driven decisions and optimise their advertising campaigns for better results.

Changing consumer behaviour

The rise of digital media has changed consumer behaviour as more people consume news, entertainment, and information online. They can instantly compare news from different media houses and instantly switch between topics. Many have opted out of the traditional methods of reading the news or watching television. Traditional media houses have struggled to adapt to this shift in consumer behaviour, as their business models are often based on print or broadcast media, where customer loyalty is essential.

In contrast, user experience becomes more important in the digital world. Irrespective of what you are trying to sell, your customer segment has more options; hence, their behaviour is bound to change. You have to learn to adapt to the changing behaviour.

Data Analytics

Digital media giants have a significant advantage in data analytics, as they can collect and analyse vast amounts of data on consumer behaviour, preferences, and interests. This allows them to deliver highly targeted and personalised content and advertising, which is difficult for traditional media houses to replicate as they still are not used to leveraging data-based AI tools to do that. The same is true for any shopping portal.

Customers may not always know their options while buying a product. The study has found that by suggesting what other customers have purchased, many would look at those options, and some would buy them. Product sales have increased by up to 30% through these suggestions.

Things like this have resulted in a shift of advertising dollars from traditional to digital media as businesses seek to reach their target audiences more effectively. However, one must understand that our perception of digital media's impact and value-for-money advertising may not be entirely true.

When I worked for IBM, in one of the roles I was responsible for driving usage of *developerWorks* by adding new technical articles and increasing its reach. I used the pay-per-click advertising option, and I found that the agency had put the link in places where the audience may not be relevant to our product line. So, we got many clicks, but the usage of the knowledge portal did not go up. The same can be true for many other acts of competition, which sounds very attractive but can have loopholes. So, study your new competition, learn about them, understand the weaknesses in their products or strategies, and devise your way forward.

You make your competitors' jobs easier when you do not act. When you are losing market share, look out for what the competition is doing to gain that market share and make some noise to hold on to your pie. Desperate discounting or sacking of the workforce is not the answer.

As a football player, I can tell you that you do not score goals by pulling back your forwards inside your half. Playing defensive can reduce the chances of the opponent team scoring a goal, but your team will never score a goal as they need to go beyond the half line to aim and shoot.

Collaborate

Go beyond traditional thinking on collaboration. One should be open to the idea of collaborating with competition if needed. There will be areas of common interest where both organisations can gain. When confrontation can cause more damage, explore the possibility of co-optation.

Redhat and Microsoft are competitors. If Redhat gains market share in the Linux OS business, it directly impacts Microsoft's business and vice versa. Despite this, they joined hands and allowed Redhat solutions to run on Microsoft Azure. The collaboration has proven to be a win-win for both parties. Business has increased for them.

Joint Go To Market with organisations who see value in working with you can be a good way of making noise and introducing your products and services. Leverage each other's presence and strength to grow the business.

Focus on brand strengths

Focusing on brand strength to generate visibility and make noise involves various activities. Here are some ways to achieve this:

Brand Identity: Your brand identity should be defined based on your values and achievements. Highlight your differentiators, explaining how they help solve critical customer problems through blogs, posts, or other digital content and driving the audience to your official website. You have to go beyond the product in doing so. For example, when we say Newgen is a billion-dollar valuation product company from India, it does create an impact without talking about the product or anything else.

Deliver Exceptional Customer Experience in every interaction: Positive customer experience in every aspect of sales helps. How professional your office receptionist is in receiving the call, transferring it to the right person, or getting back to the customer in case the person concerned is missing are some of the basics that are extremely important in forming an opinion about the organisation. The same is true when they visit your store or office. Secondly, how effective is your helpdesk in resolving customer problems? The sales process and every aspect of interaction matters and help increase visibility and credibility.

Encourage User-Generated Content: Encourage and incentivise customers to write reviews, articles, or white papers on your products and technology. This creates an excellent impression about you as an organisation. Put dedicated resources to work on this and build the knowledge base that will always have a positive impact on the customers.

Digital Marketing

Picking the basics is easy; however, becoming an expert to get the maximum out of it is challenging, and organisations need to build teams to execute their digital marketing strategy. Here are some steps for developing a digital marketing strategy:

Identify your potential customers and determine their demographics, preferences, and behaviours. Create a clear and compelling message that resonates with your target audience. Talk to your existing customers to know what impresses them the most. Use that in your pitch. Once you are ready with this, identify the digital media your organisation would like to leverage to spread that news.

Website: A business website is essential for establishing an online presence and providing information about the company, products, or services, and contact information.

Social media: Social media platforms, such as *Facebook*, X (formerly *Twitter*), *LinkedIn*, YouTube and *Instagram*, can engage with customers, promote products or services, and build brand awareness.

Email marketing: Email marketing is a cost-effective way to communicate with customers and prospects and can be used to promote products, share news and updates, and build customer relationships.

Search engine marketing (SEM): SEM includes both search engine optimisation (SEO) and pay-per-click (PPC) advertising and can be used to increase website traffic and visibility in search engine results. With increased internet usage, this marketing method has become a must.

SEO is optimising a website to rank higher in search engine results pages. One can also use backlinks from other partner websites to increase visibility and access to those who will search for your organisation.

Landing Page: Ensure your landing pages are optimised for conversions by including a clear call-to-action, relevant information, and a visually appealing design.

Use analytics tools to track clicks, conversions, and other metrics. Adjust your campaigns based on the data to improve performance over time.

Following these best practices and refining your strategy can improve your website's search engine rankings and drive more traffic, which can mean more business.

Partner meets to increase visibility

Partner meets can be a great way to improve camaraderie with partners and increase visibility to get their mindshare.

Before planning a partner conference, set clear goals for the meeting. This could include sharing company updates, discussing sales goals, or providing training on new products. Setting clear goals will help ensure that the meeting is focused and productive.

Plan engaging activities that allow partners to interact and build relationships. This could include team-building exercises, networking events, or social activities. Make sure to choose activities relevant to the partners and align with the goals of the meeting.

To motivate partners to work harder, announce incentives for achieving specific goals during the meet. This could include bonuses for reaching sales targets or recognition for outstanding performance. Incentives can help partners stay motivated and focused on achieving their goals.

Encourage partners to provide feedback. This feedback can be invaluable for improving the partnership and strengthening relationships.

After the meeting, follow up with partners to ensure they have all the necessary information. As a result, relationships built during the meeting will be reinforced, and the company will demonstrate its value to its partners. This will motivate the partners to go out and talk about the organisation. How you treat them will define how they will treat you in the marketplace.

Customer meets to increase mindshare

It does not matter what product you sell. You must have at least an annual meeting with your customers to share your achievements and plans. One of the simpler and more economical ways of doing customer meetings for many customers is to allow people to come and go. Serve tea, coffee, and snacks throughout the day. Some agenda items can be repetitive so that different audience segments can come at different times to listen to them. This is a subtle way of making noise and increasing reach and visibility.

Team outing is a must

Making noise internally inside your organisation is equally important, if not more. Ensure they are getting the message and internalising it. You want each one of them to be your loudspeaker. Every employee counts. So, make sure they work as a team and take pride in it so that each of them goes beyond the call of duty and makes noise to increase visibility and business even when they do not work with you. Make the outing memorable. Soft power matters.

Cross-functional team outings can be essential for building a cohesive team and maintaining morale. Team outings can help team members get to know each other personally and build stronger relationships. This can help improve team communication and collaboration, leading to higher productivity and better results.

Team outings can be a way to recognise and appreciate team members' hard work and contributions. The concept of 100 percent clubs is primarily to recognise and reward those sales team members who have achieved 100 percent of their sales targets in that financial year. This can help build a sense of pride and loyalty to the team and company. Most SMB organisations do not believe in having such clubs. Think about it as it can be a step in the right direction.

Spending marketing dollars

Considering the rise of the international giants in the digital print media, it can be a good opportunity for those who want to leverage traditional newspapers and news magazines to reach out to potential customers. Organisations can negotiate a comprehensive advertising deal with popular print media houses. They can request a complete package including TV, print media, and digital media.

Most small and mid-sized firms may not have enough budgets for marketing. Hence, we need to find a way to run a low-cost grassroots marketing campaign.

Identify the target audience based on demography, interest, pain points, and delivery capability.

Highlight a unique, or at the most two, value proposition which will resonate with the target audience. Use social media platforms like *LinkedIn*, *Facebook*, *Instagram*, X (*Twitter*), etc. to promote for free and even explore the paid options depending on your budget.

Collaborate with your local partners and do joint promotion campaigns. You can promote each other in your campaigns and help each other grow. Similarly, you can organise co-hosted events.

Participate in local exhibitions wherever possible. Organise industry-focused workshops or webinars to benefit the customers and also promote your products and services.

You can also explore something bold, unusual and different, like doing a flash mob or a quick fashion show in a business area or at an industry event. This is like guerrilla marketing. Short and swift but impactful.

Encourage satisfied customers to share their experiences via reviews, testimonials, or social media posts. Engage with industry-relevant magazines and help them with your content in a way that they would like to talk about using your products and services as examples.

Breaking bread with customers

One can do extended breakfast or lunch and dinner meetings to discuss ways of doing business with your potential customers. You can invite some of the select existing customers for a face-to-face meeting with the senior folks of the organisation. This can be to discuss specific issues, or it can be to do a generic messaging on new things on which the organisation is working. Do not do any forced selling in such meetings.

Seminars and workshops

There are different ways of organising them. Organisations should see what works better for them based on time, place, technical resources, and funding availability. An economical yet effective way of doing it is organising both things on the same day. In the first half, have a session with senior leadership explaining your products and solutions, customer benefits, and some case studies. Keep it brief and keep it focussed. In the second half, organise a hands-on workshop for actual product users. Help them get a natural feel of the product or solution, giving them the confidence to buy.

Organising such workshops along with industry events can have an added advantage. Industry events can get the needed captive audience.

14
CHAPTER

Be Ethical

This chapter is about why being ethical in business is super important. It's about the nuts and bolts of running a successful business. Being moral isn't just about being nice; it's about making smart moves to help your business thrive instead of tanking. Let's break it down: Being ethical can make your business grow and make it significant when things get tough. Trust me, it's worth it.

Lack of ethics and integrity can be attributed to several factors; however, the biggest reason is the lack of enough resources to grow the business. The pressure to cut costs can compromise the quality of work. Organisations also compromise on the quality of the people they hire.

Second, the informal work environment adds to this problem. When there are no standard rules and people work and get work done based on relationships instead of a formally defined process, it becomes difficult to monitor improper practices. Unethical practices and lack of integrity go unchecked.

When employees develop the habit of following unethical practices, they also lose integrity towards the organisation. It becomes their habit to follow corrupt practices even inside the organisation. Individual welfare and gain become more important than organisational growth and stability.

Throughout history, the fate of kings and empires worldwide has been intricately tied to the ethical conduct of their ruling elite. Countless historical examples illustrate this perilous path of ethical erosion and its catastrophic consequences.

In the case of 'The French Revolution and the Court of Louis XVI'. The opulent court of Louis XVI of France, marked by extravagance and indifference to the suffering of the masses, became a breeding ground for discontent and revolution.

Eventually, the masses, enraged by the daily struggle, revolted against the mighty empire. The empire crashed, and the king and his confidantes had to run to hide. All those caught were killed—a sad ending to such a great empire.

Similarly, when customers feel exploited and struggle in a business organisation, the business also starts struggling to grow. The result is bare survival or closure. This is when they should have galloped to the next level.

Organisations need to understand the root causes and take appropriate action to address unethical behaviour among salespeople. This could include providing proper training on ethical practices and holding employees accountable for unethical behaviour.

Organisations can maintain a positive image and protect their business by addressing the root causes of unethical behaviour and promoting a culture of ethics and integrity.

Salespeople may need to meet their sales targets and earn commissions, which can create pressure to use unethical sales tactics to close deals. The customer-facing teams may not even understand how their acts are evil and how they can impact them and the organisation.

This also happens partly because the company culture emphasises results at any cost. This encourages salespeople to prioritise their interests over those of the customer, leading to unethical behaviour. One common reason for engaging in unethical practice is for personal gain.

Unethical behaviour can have negative consequences for both customers and the organisation. Employees who engage in unethical behaviour can harm the organisation's reputation, contribute to financial losses, and damage internal relationships.

Unethical behaviour can be a slippery slope, where individuals who engage in such behaviour may become emboldened and more likely to engage in it again. This can lead to a culture of dishonesty within the organisation, with employees feeling that such behaviour is acceptable or expected.

Establishing clear values and expectations around ethical behaviour within an organisation is essential for preventing unethical behaviour. This should be communicated clearly to all employees and reinforced through training, policies, and procedures.

Organisations should also establish mechanisms for reporting and addressing unethical behaviour and a process for investigating and addressing reported incidents.

By establishing a culture of ethics and accountability, organisations can help prevent unethical behaviour and protect themselves from financial losses and reputational damage.

Monitor and address unethical behaviour

Companies can establish clear guidelines for ethical practices and provide employees with a code of conduct or ethics policy to follow. This can help clarify what is and is not acceptable behaviour.

In IBM we had Business Conduct Guidelines. Three violations meant termination of service. This ensured that everyone followed the guidelines sincerely.

Do your homework

A trained sales and pre-sales resource may handle a customer's need more intelligently, reducing the chance of telling lies. This means that one should plan before any important call, even if the purpose of the call is to explore the next steps. Planning can help people be more prepared and confident during the call, improving their chances of success.

A culture of ethical behaviour in sales will reduce the risk of sales returns or getting sued by customers because of unethical selling.

Handling customers

Demanding customers can pressure customer-facing teams to make overcommitments, which can ultimately harm the relationship with the customer and create bigger problems for the organisation. Hence training on managing difficult customer conversations, setting realistic expectations, and handling situations where the customer demands more than the organisation can deliver is important.

It's also essential for the sales team to proactively address potential issues with demanding customers. This means engaging in open and honest communication with the customer, setting clear expectations, and working collaboratively to find solutions that meet the customer's needs and the organisation's capabilities.

Avoiding difficult discussions or postponing problems can worsen the situation, as the customer may become increasingly frustrated and disappointed with the organisation's response. Instead, the client management team should proactively manage customer expectations, address concerns as they arise, and work collaboratively with the customer to find mutually beneficial solutions.

How to prepare for important calls

To avoid getting under stress during calls with the customer, prepare yourself thoroughly for every important call. Salespeople seldom do this; hence it is emphasised here in the book.

Define the purpose of the call: A salesperson should clearly understand the purpose of the call and what they hope to achieve. This can help to stay focused and on track during the call.

Prepare a call agenda: Research the customer and then prepare an agenda for the call, outlining the key points to be covered and the questions to ask. This can help stay organised and ensure that all important topics are addressed.

Anticipate objections: A salesperson should anticipate any objections or concerns that the prospect may raise during the call and prepare responses to address them, and this will help build confidence and identify any areas that need improvement.

Lack of exposure and experience

Why do you think people overcommit even when they are not habitual liars and do not intend to commit more than they can honour? Still, many salespersons walk out of the meeting, committing things they do not know how to honour.

The saying, do not send sheep to negotiate with jackals, cautions against sending inexperienced or unprepared negotiators to negotiate with experienced and aggressive counterparts.

Organisations need to identify and train salespeople to handle complex negotiations. This should include providing training on negotiation techniques, developing a deep understanding of the organisation's products and services, and preparing for potential challenges and objections. They should be taught how to win deals without always agreeing on every customer demand. How can this help save a project, and why is all this important?

Customers become demanding not because they need everything; they become demanding when the salespeople start agreeing on everything even when it is not there. Just for a moment, imagine you going out to buy a two-bedroom apartment at a given cost, and you realise during the discussion that if you push it hard, you can get a four-bedroom apartment at the same cost. What will you do? Usually, push it for four bedrooms even though that was not the initial plan. The same is true for any customer.

Ultimately, the key to successful negotiations is preparation and skills.

Sell what you have

The statement, sell what you have and not what you wish you had, means that it is essential to be realistic and practical when making sales. It suggests that it is important to focus on your products or services and their benefits rather than on what you wish you had or what you think would be great to offer. However, if you are in the consulting business, then this rule may not be applicable as you are primarily selling a dream which you think can be achieved in a given time within a given budget.

When we try to sell something that we do not have but the customer thinks we have, we are essentially selling a dream or an illusion, which can often lead to disappointment, frustration, and, ultimately, failure. This approach can also harm our reputation and credibility as a seller, making it harder for us to succeed in the long term.

Even in the manufacturing or trading business, many commit to the wrong delivery timeline without bothering about the consequences or the problems the customer will face because of these wrong commitments on the delivery timeline. The problem can be because of a lack of product or raw material availability or many other things affecting the supply chain. This creates bad blood with your customers, spoiling relationships and putting the future business in jeopardy many times. Avoid giving bad surprises.

On the other hand, when we focus on what we have, we can present our products or services in a more authentic and genuine way and define our delivery timelines in a realistic manner. This approach allows us to build trust and credibility with our customers, which can lead to repeat business and positive word-of-mouth referrals.

Be honest with your customers
No customer likes to feel cheated and, once cheated, may not like to revisit the same shop again. Still, it is common not to be transparent with customers. It's important to be honest with the customer and inform them if your product will not do everything that they are expecting or that you will be trying something for the first time; hence, hiccups in execution are expected. Instead of losing the deal you may have a customer for life. Transparency and clear communication with the customer are key to

building long-lasting relationships and trust. Let the customer know in advance so that they can understand the risks involved and set their expectations accordingly. This can help avoid misunderstandings or disappointment if the project takes longer or does not turn out as expected.

By being upfront about your experience level and skills, you demonstrate your honesty and integrity to the customer, which can help build a strong foundation for a successful business relationship.

Honesty can make selling a bit difficult in the initial phase, more so in developing economies. So, try to be as honest as practically possible.

15
CHAPTER

What is Your Story

A compelling story is an essential aspect of marketing and selling a product or service. A good story can help customers connect with a brand on an emotional level, which can ultimately lead to increased loyalty and sales.

A story which can help build a positive image by highlighting the differentiating factors in a way which appeals to the thought process of the customer and the way the employees carry themselves in their interactions with people inside the organization or outside the organization can make a huge difference.

In addition, a good story can help to build trust with customers by showcasing the authenticity and integrity of a company. By sharing the human elements behind a brand, such as the people and values that drive it, customers are more likely to view the brand as trustworthy and relatable.

Ultimately, a company's story should be authentic, compelling, and aligned with its brand identity and values. A strong brand story can be a powerful tool for engaging customers and driving sales.

Build a positive image

A positive image can help a company to attract and retain customers, recruit top talent, and build strong relationships with stakeholders.

There are many ways to build a positive image for an organisation. Some of the important things that can help and guide any organisation interested in doing so are listed below.

Avoid overcommitting: Delivering high-quality products or services that meet or exceed customer expectations can be the first one. Ensure that your sales team does not oversell the product and that your delivery team does not overcommit on the deliverables. There is a market for all kinds of products and solutions; hence, one can sell even without overcommitting. Do not allow this culture to grow in the organisation. It adds a lot of unwanted stress and creates unhappy customers and unhappy employees. The easiest way to control this temptation is by highlighting the mistake to the employee concerned every time they do it and helping them understand the potential loss the company can have because of that behaviour. Things will not change overnight, but they will change.

Control the presumptuous types: People in the organisation tend to show that they know everything and, hence, discuss things with customers that they should not. This creates more problems than it solves.

A pharmaceutical company developed a product for a critical disease and had it tested by the healthcare department. A senior director asked the representative about the possible price of the product. They wanted the price lower so that even poor patients could buy it, and the government could buy it in bulk. A representative who had no idea about the pricing suggested that the price should be in the range of ₹20 to ₹30. An estimate of about ₹350 was sent to the government after the product was certified. The senior director got very upset and secured final approval of ₹108 per piece instead of ₹350.

Despite the urgent requirement, nothing changed even after a few months since the perception that the price would be much lower created all the confusion. Wrong communication creates a negative image that impacts sales. This is a real incidence.

Corporate social responsibility: Giving back to the community through corporate social responsibility initiatives also helps create a positive image. Organising free training for academia on the latest technologies is a popular mode of giving back to society. It helps build a positive impression. Many organiations run a separate division to address the academia. Some give free training material too and some offer the product at a highly discounted price.

Online presence: Maintain a strong online presence through social media, blogs, and other digital platforms that engage customers and promote the brand. Involve your partners and customers to contribute to this activity. When customers talk positively and post it online, it creates a positive, feel-good factor and helps build trust and sell your product or service.

The differentiating factor

Ultimately, identifying and leveraging the factors that set a company apart from its competitors is the key to creating an impact in the market. By developing a strong brand identity, prioritising customer experience and innovation, and engaging in socially responsible practices, companies can differentiate themselves and create a competitive advantage in the marketplace.

A well-designed pricing strategy can also differentiate, as companies that offer competitive prices or unique pricing models can attract and retain customers.

For example, take the cost of an *Enterprise Linux* operating system. While working for *SCO Unix*, we competed with *Linux*-selling organisations. People knew that *Linux* is open source and hence, available for free. However, the free version was different from the *Enterprise* version. In many cases, the *Enterprise* version was as expensive as the commercial versions of competing operating systems. However, the thought process among the masses that the software is free created a strong brand perception, and we had a tough time competing with them in the marketplace, even though SCO Unix was technically, then, a superior product with an extensive user base. SCO did not go down in a day, and neither Linux OS became popular overnight. Not many may know that when Red Hat Linux and SUSE Linux were gaining popularity and capturing market share, there were close to another 100 plus Linux operating systems, which were mostly available for free but were not getting picked up by the users. Price alone cannot be the differentiating factor. So, why is it that established products start losing out to new entrants. Why the customers start switching ?

Appeal to the thought process of customers

Appealing to the thought process of customers is important to drive business. Messages and marketing efforts should be tailored to customers' needs and desires in order to resonate with them. Several strategies can be employed to achieve this.

Emphasising benefits: Customers want to know how a product or service will benefit them. By highlighting the specific benefits relevant to the customer that a product or service provides, companies can appeal to customers' thought processes and demonstrate how their offerings can solve their problems or meet their needs.

Creating emotional connections: Emotions can play an influential role in decision-making. By creating emotional connections with customers through storytelling, empathetic messaging, and relatable content, companies can appeal to the thought process of customers and create a sense of connection that can lead to increased engagement and loyalty. The fact that Linux was open source, created by the people, for the people and available for free was a great motivating factor, even though, in reality, the free version had no support available and a few other things were missing. It appealed to the masses. They like the concept of community support even when you cannot run mission-critical applications or important office applications on community support, which may help or may not.

Leveraging social proof: Social proof, such as customer reviews, testimonials, and case studies, can help to build trust with customers and demonstrate the value of a product or service.

All this, when done repetitively using catchy slogans and taglines, should help improve the recall value of the product or service. That should help in increasing sales.

Walk tall

Organisations need to encourage their staff to walk tall and be proud of their work and the organisation where they work. Employees who feel proud and engaged in their work are more likely to be motivated, productive, and committed to the organisation's success. This helps in closing more deals.

Fostering a positive workplace culture helps create an environment where employees feel valued, supported, and engaged. This can be achieved by promoting open communication, recognising and rewarding employee achievements, and fostering a sense of teamwork and collaboration.

Encouraging employees to walk tall and take pride in their work is essential for creating a positive workplace culture and driving organisational success. One can see that the impact of this gives your employees the needed courage to do tough negotiations better. This also helps ensure that they will overcommit much less, leading to increased customer satisfaction.

As we conclude this chapter, remember that your story is not just about your company but your impact on your audience and the world. Building a positive image through ethical practices, inclusivity, and a commitment to societal well-being is good for business; it reflects your values. So, refine your storytelling skills and embark on a journey to create a lasting and meaningful impression.

16

CHAPTER

Sales Closure and Happy Customers

In any sales pipeline, the biggest challenge is to get the closures. Sales closure refers to finalising a sale by getting the customer to commit to purchasing a product or service. It is the point where a salesperson secures a deal and converts a potential customer into an actual customer.

The method of selling will vary depending on the type of sales your organisation is involved in. A mass-selling product will need a different approach than an enterprise product; however, some factors will be the same. Similarly, selling in a market where people know the brand versus selling in a market where people do not know the brand will also require different approaches.

When I lived in Mumbai in 1993, I used to witness a sale happening in 40 seconds. The deal followed the usual sales cycle of suspect to collection and delivery. However, the example is perfect for helping explain the steps in a sales closure.

When the local train entered the platform of Matunga Central at around 8 pm, it took five seconds to slow down, and that is when this sales process started. The cauliflower salesperson, a young boy around 12 years old, started looking at the potential suspects for sale. His products were usually of good quality and not very cheap, so he always went after the first-class compartment to sell. It was the Sales Stage 1, where you identify the market segment which you want to address to sell your product. He quickly identified the potential customer among those sitting or standing on the train based on their interest in listening to him. The shortlisted people became prospects, where he thought the chance of selling was high. He was now in the Sales Stage 2 and was running along with one of the windows he had identified to make the sale happen. You identify and shortlist potential customers who respond to your marketing campaign in any business.

The train stopped for 30 seconds. The boy demonstrated the product, which in this case was cauliflower. He went ahead with his crisp elevator pitch to impress upon the customer. The pitch was well rehearsed so he could rattle down the pitch with the needed emotions and sentiments, thereby giving a personal touch to the potential sale. This was Sales Stage 3. The price negotiation started with a potential customer showing maximum interest. The customer started bargaining for a better offer. This was Sales Stage 4.

The customer he was targeting decided not to go ahead with the purchase. He disagreed on the price. The sales boy was slightly heartbroken and tried to revive the situation. The case had reached Sales Stage 0. He quickly shifted his focus to the next eager person looking at him. This potential customer had also heard the elevator pitch and had seen the demonstration of the product; therefore, the round of negotiation started.

He was back to Sales Stage 4. The salesperson started pushing for the closure. He had only five seconds left before the train would start moving again. The fear of losing a good purchase, the convincing pitch, and the demo made the customer buy the cauliflower at the agreed rate. This was Sales Stage 5. The Sales boy holding the cauliflower delivered the product to the customer.

The train started moving now. The collection was still pending, and the eagerness to close the deal did not deter him from pushing the customer to make the payment. He asked for the money even when the delivery process had not started. He gets the money in five seconds, or it's a direct loss. Pricing was designed so that customers wouldn't struggle with currency notes. The customer takes out the payment and hands the cash to the sales boy, who is holding the railing of the train's window and running with him. The collection was done. This was Sales Stage 6. Even in business, customers who decide to buy usually have the necessary financial arrangements to make the payment. So, one needs to think about why they delay the payments and, at times, don't pay at all. Where did the seller go wrong?

A successful sale was made in 40 seconds. the sequence was followed meticulously by the seller and buyer, and this happened every day. If this was a corporate business, how would the team analyse the business to have more closures and grow the business further?

One faces a similar situation in most sales scenarios. A professional sales team will analyse this and strategise to scale up the business or increase the chance of making more sales every 40 seconds. This will include looking into the backend process of procuring the quality material in bulk at a reasonable price so that no objections are raised on the quality front and can be sold at a competitive price, thereby holding on to the existing customer base. They could add more sales staff to sell as there is a scope to deploy one person in every bogey, and in a local train, one can have 12 to 14 bogeys. This is analysing the potential to sell and adding extra foot on the street. They can check if one really needs any pitch in such a sale or only price and quality, and reaching out to the customer will do. One needs to have a holistic approach in any business to see which areas one needs to improve upon to close faster and grow the business. Do not just depend on the salesperson.

Copying the same sales strategy may not work on long-distance trains or people travelling long distances, say, from Mumbai to Delhi or Kolkata, as they may not be interested in buying vegetables on the way. So, selecting the geography and understanding the customer's purpose are equally important to making a sale happen.

Let us stick to this example to understand how strategies fail or how performers become nonperformers by not closing enough deals. In the corporate world, such tactics are common, sometimes done wilfully and sometimes by mistake. A performer may be tasked with selling cauliflower at the stations where air-conditioned trains stop to pick up passengers or where long-distance trains stop. The basic assumptions to make a sale happen change completely in such a situation as customers, even if interested, may not be able to buy sitting in an air-conditioned coach. Suppose the sales team's performance working in such train stations is compared with the person selling in Matunga or any such train station where local trains stop, and what will the outcome be? The performance difference will be huge. Unfortunately, when you copy a strategy blindly without understanding the ground rules and without doing the basic analysis, sales will always suffer, and closures will be challenging. This example illustrates that the success of sales depends on the suitability of the product to the territory, not only the sales team's capability.

Addressing any customer's objections is another way of pushing a deal towards closure, provided the salesperson has understood the problem and can satisfy the customer's request. It is a good habit to ask for a commitment to buy before solving all problems. A willing customer may not hesitate to commit; however, those who are experimenting or using this opportunity for self-learning may come out with their side of the truth. So, it helps to know if you should expect closure or do the work for a good future pipeline or one is only creating awareness. Organisations can do separate awareness session for such customers separately.

Presenting the product or service's benefits, which will help the customer and is needed by the customer, is also vital to show value. Often, customers are so used to working in the traditional style that they do not realise there can be solutions to problems they do not even know. When you live with a concern for too long, you accept that as a way of life and start living with it. The *iPhone* changed the perception people had about a smartphone. The touch screen of the *iPhone* showed customers what they were missing. The introduction of the concept of a modular kitchen was a revolutionary experience for many people, completely transforming the way kitchens were designed and constructed. While some experiences are best conveyed visually, in other cases, it is crucial to explain things thoroughly and accurately.

Finally, creating a sense of urgency to encourage the customer to decide is difficult in some cases and easy in others. When the Indian government announced that income from insurance policies would now have a tax component if the policy was not bought by 31 March 2023, there was a mad rush to buy insurance. Unprecedented sales were witnessed.

Similarly, in the late 80s, when the government announced section 32AB of the Income Tax Act, which helped organisations save tax by investing in IT, many customers started buying personal computers. However, not every salesperson used that as an excuse to help customers buy. Not everyone knew about it.

Similarly, capital expense versus operational expense can also help some customers make a faster decision. Does the salesperson know about this? Is he bringing up this point in their discussion with the Chief Financial Officer? These things are beyond your product or solution but help expedite the sales process. So, keep looking for such opportunities to help your team sell more.

Check a few basic things in every sale to understand whether the customer will buy the product. These four things are 'need' for the product should exist, 'acceptance' of the fact that the product will do what they need, they have the defined 'budget' to invest and if there is a 'timeline' defined for buying the product.

When progression stops

Usually, after reaching a stage in the sales cycle, the cases stop progressing. This means many customers initially show interest but slowly lose it for various reasons. On online shopping portals, you will see many people who have identified things they want to buy; some were also put in the payment cart, but no decision was taken.

This means that customers need help in making a decision. Hence, organisations need to understand the potential reasons and run campaigns to help them decide. Helping the customer make a favourable decision is a lead progression campaign and is important to drive that extra revenue.

Interaction with the customer

A significant reason for losing a deal almost custom-made for your product and solution needs root cause analysis. One reason could be wrong pitching. This means the customer never understood the product's real strength. The other reason could be that the customer is not able to trust that what is getting promised will actually be delivered. Finally in some cases the customer can have a vested interest in buying the product from someone else.

Features versus benefits

While features highlight what a product or service can do, benefits focus on how they directly address the customers' needs and solve their problems. Effectively conveying the benefits ensures that customers understand how the product is solving their problem, and that makes it easier for the customer to make a favourable buying decision.

The sale may never happen if you start with features and the customer finds it difficult to relate.

Demonstrate the power

Assuming that your competition is more popular, more visible, and more known than you, the salesperson's job becomes slightly more complex. Spend time understanding the gap that the intense competition has left open and which you fill well. Just emphasise that. A gap always exists. If you look for it long enough, you will find it. When you cannot beat the competition on price and features, then focus on relationships and support. Spend time with the customer to understand their pain points and explain how your organisation can help the customer better without naming the competition. The more you name the competition, the more is the brand recall, so avoid that. Focus on your strengths and success stories. You should meet multiple people in the organisation. Understand their role in the organisation and their role in the buying process and help them understand your value proposition. If there are multiple deals managed by an individual where regular meetings may not be possible, build automated tools and standardise methods to reach out to the customers and use local business partners to give personal touch to make sales happen. The personal touch helps in winning the trust and in winning deals. Even in web portal-based sales, one must find places where customers can visit, touch and feel the product. Alternatively, give them enough documents and video support to give them near real-life experience.

When I came to *Newgen* from *IBM*, I realised that the former had grown organically as a software company. Hence, in one solution line, *Newgen* had all their components or software products that could efficiently work together or independently per the customer's need, whereas doing the same at *IBM* was a big challenge. This proved to be a game changer for the Channel team in many opportunities. Knowledge about your competition helps. So, next time you go for a customer meeting, explore how competitive products are being used and the existing gaps which exist, which can be exploited to win deals.

Once the customer buys and uses your product, work towards cementing the relationship. Put a focused team of experienced relationship managers on the job to ensure customer delight and make them put a good word for your product and organisation. Take help from the same team to spread out in that organisation. Most big established players follow this strategy effectively. However, many small and medium-sized organisations fail to follow this strategy. They usually stick to one sale and one department, slowing their growth and helping the competition get in. The successfully running solution works like a proof of concept for the organisation. This creates a potential for more such solutions.

Listening to your customers

Effective listening and understanding your customer's needs and concerns can make a significant difference in building trust and forming a strong business relationship.

Encourage your customers to express themselves by asking open-ended questions that require more than a simple 'yes' or 'no' answer. Put yourself in your customers' shoes to understand their perspectives better.

Take notes of essential points raised by the customer. It shows that you value their input and helps you recall critical details later.

Objection handling is an art, and one can learn to handle delays and customer objections only with enough practice. Salespeople try to win the debate and lose the deal. If a customer has objected, spend some time understanding the complaint, and in case of doubt, ask for clarification. Also, do not hesitate to involve your other relevant team members who can help address the issues better. Once the customer stops complaining, do not think that the problem has been resolved. Many customers may not complain again and decide not to buy your product or service.

Market coverage

A small team can cover a big geography in less-served markets. However, the bigger the market, the more the competition, and you need better preparedness to win market share. So, avoid spreading thin. Pick your geography and focus there.

As a new entrant in a developed market, a small team of one or two people trying to sell and make a mark usually struggles if they are an unknown brand name. They slowly start losing confidence and find it difficult to sell. Facing failure for too long is not good for morale, which translates into poor sales. So, rotating teams or adding new members with needed experience and exposure will help keep the confidence high and assist in selling.

Managing competition

Managing competition is an essential part of winning any deal. Competition is fierce in today's business world, and customers have many options. As a result, businesses need to be able to differentiate themselves from their competitors and effectively manage the competition to win deals. A small list of guiding principles has been defined to help you win.

Understand the competition: The first step in managing competition is understanding who your competitors are and what they offer. This can help you differentiate yourself and position your product or service more effectively. Avoid going by hearsay, as the rumours can help the competition win, rather spend time fact-finding and putting together your plan to counter them.

Focus on your unique selling proposition (USP): By focusing on your USP, you can emphasise your value to the customer and differentiate yourself from your competitors. Do not allow competition to define the ground rules.

In hockey, when the Western countries realised that they could not win against India in the standard field, they created *AstroTurf*-based playgrounds. The ball behaved differently, and countries like India lost their dominance in the game. Between 1928 and 1980, India won gold medals for hockey in Olympics around eight times. Then *Astroturf* was introduced, and India could not win even once after that. This is the kind of impact you can have by changing the ground rules of the competition.

Acknowledge the strengths and weaknesses of the competition, and show the customer why your product or service is better. Study competition and the application of their products and solutions to solve customer problems. If you find weaknesses, then expose them. If you do not find any weakness, you have not worked hard enough.

Build strong relationships with customers: Building solid relationships can help you win deals, even if your competitors have similar products or services. Customers choose a business they trust and feel a connection with. Hence, meet them and give them the needed confidence. Meet all people concerned and not just one willing to talk.

Managing competition is essential to winning deals; businesses must be proactive to stay ahead.

Performance dashboard KPIs

Dashboards are helpful in measurement. Without measurement, it isn't easy to monitor real progress. A performance dashboard with the right KPIs (key performance indicators) can be an effective tool for understanding why sales are winning or losing deals.

Here are some KPIs that could be useful in a performance dashboard.

Deal pipeline: Measure the number of deals the sales team is working on and number of deals which are actually progressing.

A large pipeline can often make you complacent. So, a conversion ratio supported by previous performance data can be helpful in getting the true picture of potential closures, which are possible.

Win/loss ratio: This KPI measures the number of deals won versus the number of opportunities lost. This can help businesses understand the effectiveness of their sales team in winning contracts and identify areas for improvement. This should also be done considering the size of the addressable market, the help given to sales teams, as it can vary from one geography to another. Evaluate the reason for success and attempt to replicate the process which helped win deals.

Deal size: What is the average deal size witch the sales team is closing? Increase the value and number of closures in a phased manner. Incentivise the team for achieving this. Every year, some progress should happen.

Time-to-close: This KPI measures the time it takes to close deals. You may like to review the new deals, renewal of deals, collection of Annual Technical Support charges and check how many cases are dropping yearly. How many customers are going away to competition? Identify the reason and work on those problem areas. This can help businesses identify bottlenecks in the sales process and take corrective actions to speed up the process.

Partner, dealer or sales agent engagement: This KPI measures the level of engagement of partners with the business, such as training sessions attended, the number of joint marketing activities, and the level of communication. This can help companies understand their partners' commitment and loyalty levels.

By tracking these KPIs, businesses can get a comprehensive view of sales performance and understand why they are winning or unable to help win deals. This can help companies identify areas for improvement and take necessary actions to improve sales performance and drive revenue growth.

Empowering account managers to become sales-focused

Empowering account managers to become more sales-focused can significantly increase revenue and drive business growth. So, how do you make a productive person more productive?

Offer incentives: Offering bonuses or commissions for achieving sales targets in lean periods can motivate account managers to focus on sales and drive results. Business goals should be aligned with incentives, and incentives should be fair and transparent. In IBM, they had this concept of giving 20% extra incentive in the first quarter for many years. This was done to counter the problem of low sales in the first quarter. This motivated the sales teams to run with extra vigour in the first quarter to take advantage of this policy.

Encourage collaboration: Collaboration between different teams and leveraging each other's strengths can also foster a culture of teamwork and drive better results. One can even do teaming with external vendors whose products or solutions are part of the overall solution you are trying to sell.

Provide the right tools: Providing account managers with the right tools, such as CRM software, sales enablement resources, and marketing collateral, can help them be more effective in their sales efforts. It is essential to ensure the tools are easy to use, accessible, and aligned with the sales goals.

Introduce mentors for guidance and coaching: Sales leaders and mentors play different but equally essential roles in driving sales success within an organisation, mainly when guiding and supporting sales teams to achieve their goals. Mentors do not carry sales targets.

Sales leaders drive the organisation's overall sales strategy and performance. They set goals, create plans, and make decisions impacting the sales team.

On the other hand, sales mentors are typically senior salespeople who guide and support the sales team. They act as a resource for advice and share their expertise and knowledge. Sales mentors can help sales representatives navigate complex sales scenarios and develop their skills to become more effective.

A strong sales leadership team can help organisations build a sales culture focused on success, growth, and continuous improvement.

Improving business planning and more effective QBRs

One should do a planning session once a year to define the roadmap and the broad KRAs to drive performance. During the year, there is a tendency to drift away from the roadmap for some reason. This applies to all project implementations, including the organisation's sales journey. Hence, a quarterly review session is critical to ensure that sales teams do not forget the objective and make the necessary course corrections if needed.

Set clear objectives and goals: It is essential to set clear objectives and goals for the business and ensure they align with the organisation's overall strategy. These objectives and goals should be measurable, achievable, and time-bound. The targets should be based on the geography's potential and the sales team's deployment.

Most Small and Midsize businesses lack data points to compare performance and set expectations. What addressable market is the sales team working on, and what percentage of the market are they controlling? What help is the organisation giving them to drive that number vis a vis competing organisations? Avoid discrimination between individuals or teams within the organisation, as that will impact performance.

Collection

The method of collecting payments can vary depending on the type of business. Some companies collect payments in advance, while for others, collecting payment upon delivery of the product or service milestone may make sense.

Managing Collections through VAD: A VAD or value-added distributor can handle the collections process on behalf of the business. In this case, the VAD would follow up on late payments, escalate payment issues, and provide regular reporting. A VAD is expected to pay the principal 100% in advance and keep a small percentage of the deal as their margin.

Collection post-delivery of product and solution: Ideally, one should try to get the payments in advance so that one does not have to chase customers after the delivery of the product or solution. Many organisations have collapsed when they could not collect the pending payments in time. When one does not have enough customers, one becomes desperate and agrees to unfavourable payment terms.

Set clear payment terms: Before providing any material or service, it's important to set clear payment terms with the customer. This can include payment deadlines, late payment fees, and payment methods. Many salespeople are afraid or too timid to discuss payment terms. Hence, a system should be in place that will ensure that a customer learns about the terms automatically without the intervention of any person who interacts with the customer.

Send invoices promptly: Once the material or service has been provided, the business should send an invoice to the customer as soon as possible. Delayed, lost, or misplaced invoices are also reasons for payment delays. So, a system should be designed to address these fundamental issues that can impact the cash flow.

Follow up on late payments: If the customer does not pay by the deadline, it's important to follow up promptly to remind them of the payment and any late payment fees. Do not hesitate to blacklist customers who do not pay on time, irrespective of the business size you get from them. You must look at the cost of collecting the payment and decide if it is worth doing business with them.

Monitor payment trends: By monitoring payment trends, businesses can identify areas where collections processes can be improved. For example, give a cash discount for paying in advance, send a proforma invoice to process the payment in advance, or get separate written commitments from senior people to ensure you get your payment in time.

Milestone-based collection: Milestone-based collections are a type of payment structure where payments are tied to the completion of specific milestones or deliverables. This approach is often used in projects where the work is complex, involves multiple stages, and may take an extended period to complete. One challenge is that customers may not pay as per the milestone but expect the deliverables to happen. Another challenge could be that the milestones are so vague that it would be as good as not having any. Walk through the simulated process and try to set a neutral system that works for both the customer and the vendor. Both organizations should establish escalation metrics in case the terms of the agreement are violated.

Issuing a letter of credit: A letter of credit (LC) is a financial instrument facilitating smooth transactions between buyers and sellers. A seller may use an LC to ensure they receive payment for goods or services provided to a buyer. The buyer's bank issues the LC to the seller's bank, promising to make payment upon fulfilling certain conditions and supplying needed documents. In some way, this guarantees the seller's payment and ensures that the buyer does not need to pay for the wrong shipment. LC is very commonly used in international business.

Managing customer expectations
Happy customers are good for business. Managing customer expectations is a crucial aspect of running a successful business. Customers have certain expectations about the products or services they purchase. When not met,

they will likely become dissatisfied and may not return. What should organisations do to manage customer expectations?

Transparency: Ensure your customers know what to expect from your products or services. Be transparent about any limitations, deadlines, or potential issues they may encounter.

Realistic expectations: Only promise what you can deliver. Set realistic expectations and ensure you have the resources and capabilities to meet them. Once you wilt under pressure, which can be internal or external, the snowball effect leading to a possible disaster is immediately put in motion unknowingly. So, learn to manage pressure and remain realistic.

Salespeople often believe that telling the truth does not work; hence, they avoid discussing contentious issues. Make that discussion mandatory as part of the process and monitor it. Slowly, things will fall into place. It takes time to ensure this, but it usually works in favour of all parties concerned.

Never stop communicating: Keep your customers informed about the status of their orders or projects. Inform them of delays or issues that may impact their expectations. Irrespective of how bad the situation is and how angry the customer will be after knowing the ground reality, never avoid or stop communicating with the customer.

Honest and good customer service: If your customers have a positive experience interacting with your business, they are more likely to have realistic expectations and be satisfied with the outcome.

Manage complaints with empathy: If a customer is unhappy with the products or services they receive, listen to their concerns, and address them as quickly as possible. This will help manage their expectations in the future and may turn a negative experience into a positive one.

Happy customers are good for business. Satisfied customers are more likely to return to your company and make repeat purchases.

Reduced marketing costs: Happy customers can help reduce marketing costs by generating positive reviews and referrals, which can help attract new customers without the need for expensive marketing campaigns.

Happy customers are essential for the success of any business. They can help generate repeat business, positive word-of-mouth marketing, increased sales, improved reputation, and reduced marketing costs.

With the right amount of consideration paid to all the factors, big and small, that affect these outcomes, you can increase your rate of sales closures and ensure happy customers at the same time.

17
CHAPTER

Diversity in the Sales Team

Diversity in sales teams is essential and relevant in today's world. A diverse sales team can bring various perspectives, experiences, and skills to the table, which can help drive innovation, creativity, and problem-solving. Additionally, having a diverse team can help build better relationships with customers from different backgrounds and cultures. If you plan to establish a national sales team in India, it is crucial to ensure participation from all regions of India. The team should have representatives from Eastern India, including the Northeast, Southern India, Western India, and people from the North. Each of these regions has its unique perspective on life and different problem-solving approaches. Therefore, having a diverse team can help bring in varied ideas and enhance the overall performance of the team.

Studies have shown that businesses with more women in leadership positions tend to have higher profitability and better financial performance than those with fewer women. This can be attributed to various factors, including diversity of perspectives, improved decision-making, better employee engagement, improved customer relations and better corporate social responsibility. Women are often more focused on social and environmental issues and are more likely to prioritise corporate social responsibility and sustainability. However, some organisations strictly believe in hiring top leadership positions based on merit and not on any other criteria.

A study conducted by *McKinsey* found that companies in the top quartile for gender diversity were 21% more likely to experience above-average profitability than companies in the bottom quartile. Another study by the *Peterson Institute for International Economics* found that companies with at least 30% female executives had a 15% increase in profitability.

Research has shown that women's leadership styles are often more collaborative and communicative, which can lead to more effective teamwork and problem-solving.

In addition, women may bring different perspectives and approaches to decision-making, which can encourage more creative thinking. For example, a study published in the *Journal of Applied Psychology* found that mixed-gender groups were more likely to generate a wider range of ideas and solutions than all-male or all-female groups.

However, it's important to note that simply having women in leadership positions is insufficient. Organisations must also create a culture that values and supports diverse perspectives and encourages open communication and collaboration. When women's voices are heard and valued, their unique perspectives can be a game changer for organisations.

When building a diverse sales team in an international business, it is essential to be mindful of local rules and regulations and the law-and-order situation in different countries. This is especially true regarding issues related to gender diversity, as women may face additional challenges in certain countries. Awareness about rules and laws related to employment, discrimination, and harassment is critical since these can vary widely from country to country. It is mandatory to research and seek legal advice as needed.

Flexibility regarding work arrangements and schedules can also help build a more diverse sales team. For example, offering flexible work hours or remote work options may be particularly helpful for women or other groups that face additional challenges in certain countries.

Across industries, it is seen that women's participation in sales roles is less than that of men. It is assumed that women are not suitable for sales roles, and in many cases, women also do not show the needed enthusiasm to start a career in sales. Diversity helps. Apart from the fact that saleswomen will stand out in a crowd of salesmen, it will be an advantage in some cases because women think differently. In many cases, they look at the same problem from a different perspective, and this is precisely what you need in any growing sales organisation.

You need different perspectives to help you better evaluate the situation and develop a winning strategy. You need to listen to them and allow them to speak. Many girls will take a back seat in a group discussion on sales. Traditionally, they have been told that sales as a career is meant for the boys. Hence, they may not speak up even if they have a better idea.

So, they may need more encouragement to speak up and more help participating in such discussions. The leader has to take it up as a project if necessary. The benefits of good participation from your female colleagues will compensate you far more than what you will invest in making them come forward and participate.

Similarly, when nurturing your existing customers to grow your business, you do not have to think only like a typical salesperson trying to sell something. You need to show the needed warmth and extend the possible help to allow them to get the maximum from what they have procured. This will help them better understand your product, which can mean more business, referrals, and happy customers.

Hiring women for a sales role is a challenge

Many believe that women candidates cannot perform as well in sales as their male counterparts. Their data proves this—you have more male CEOs than female CEOs. We forget that we also have a much smaller number of women in the workforce; hence, any such comparison from a data perspective may not do any justice to your diversity hiring program. Treat them equally and give them work of equal importance.

On more than one occasion, I have seen a tendency where the women team members are given slightly simple work and kept on the sidelines. Treating them like this breaks their self-confidence, makes them less competitive and participative in business activities, and therefore, they are able to contribute less.

Regarding customers, having women on a sales team can also help create a culture of respect towards women customers. Women make up a significant portion of the customer base, and having female sales representatives can help organisations better understand and serve their female customers' needs. By treating women customers respectfully and understanding, sales representatives can build trust and loyalty, increasing sales and customer satisfaction.

Diversity is essential while building a global sales team

Diversity in a sales team extends far beyond gender inclusion and encompasses a wide range of aspects, including hiring individuals from different nationalities, ethnicities, cultures, and backgrounds. This is especially crucial when a company intends to expand its business in various parts of the world.

When your backend team in the home country regularly works with people of different nationalities, they can better understand and appreciate their concerns. This will help teams deliver better results.

A mixed sales and marketing team can provide a better experience for various markets and customers. This can help organisations tailor their sales and marketing strategies to meet different customer segments' unique needs and preferences.

A diverse sales and marketing team can also bring cultural sensitivity and awareness. Diverse teams bring a wider range of perspectives and experiences to the table, which can lead to more creative and innovative solutions. They are also better at solving complex problems because they can draw on various experiences and expertise.

18
CHAPTER

Going Global

Cartagena, a city in Columbia, has a history of violent crimes by the drug mafia. Hence, one has to be careful in the evenings. Many Hollywood movies are based on the drug cartels of Columbia. Once in a beachside hotel in Cartagena, I and my friend and colleague, Kunal, were walking on the beach, holding a glass of Margarita on the rocks. I had a long, uncherished desire to do something like this. We had gone there to participate in an IT event. This was around 7 pm. It was not dark yet. One person in a simple, plain dress approached us. He was part of the hotel's security team.

Security: Sir, are you a guest at this hotel?

Me: Yes, we are.

Security: Sir, please walk between those two defined points. (He pointed towards two points on two sides.)

Me: Why should we do that?

Security: Sir, there are three of us on duty for the safety and protection of the guests. We are authorised to use firearms only if something happens between those two defined points. That is around a stretch of 70 to 80 metres.

Me: What happens if something happens beyond those two points?

Security: Sir, we will wait and watch till you walk back between those points. We cannot help beyond those two points.

We ended our stroll and returned to the hotel, getting used to this new reality of life. Getting surprised and accepting it as the new normal is the first prerequisite of doing business in the global market.

Going global necessitates expanding one's physical presence and cultivating a mindset ready for learning and adaptation. Stepping into unfamiliar international territories often means encountering different challenges and nuances that may vary significantly from the familiar landscape of one's home country.

These challenges are spread across cultural differences, legal issues, and market and consumer behaviours. Being mentally prepared to navigate this web of variables is critical for success. It means accepting and acknowledging that the world beyond one's home base is diverse and embracing this diversity. Going global requires a proactive willingness to learn from these differences, adapt strategies accordingly, and view each challenge as a chance to grow and thrive in the global marketplace.

In 1999, I travelled to Italy and the UAE. In both countries, we wanted to sign up with partners to do business. We followed a similar process when signing partners in these countries. We initiated discussions with potential partners from our home country. We first identified them through our secondary sources of research. We participated in GITEX in Dubai, CeBIT in Hannover and SMAU in Milan to get a first-hand feel of the market.

In Milan, we could not sign up with a partner even though we met with a few potential ones, and the market potential to do business was reasonably good. In Palermo, Sicily, my partner picked me up from the airport and dropped me off. He also had a translator to help us communicate and a gunman for our safety. The reception was very warm and friendly.

In Dubai, we initially struggled to have the right kind of partners for meetings as we could not find many partners who would understand the solutions we were trying to sell. However, we ended up doing business in the UAE while we could not progress in Italy, so we dropped that country from our list. This will happen and it showcases the differences of a well-served market and a developing and less-served market.

In a well-served market, the partners and the customers have multiple options; hence, they may not be interested in working with an unknown organisation. The effort involved in such a market is much higher. In a less-served market, the customers and partners do not have much to choose from; hence, they will be more willing to listen and explore. However, the size of the business you will do here is much less than what you can do in a well-served market, provided you succeed in breaking the entry barrier.

Growth and revenue can be increased by expanding your products and services globally. Most organisations want to go global, but they need help to succeed.

The following four aspects of sales are crucial for entering the developed markets of the USA, Europe, or other similar countries:

Competition: Analyse your local successful competitors' offerings to understand what sells and the gaps you can fill to see how you can fit in. Once you know your competitors' strengths and weaknesses, planning your approach in that market becomes easy. You can plan your offerings accordingly. It is possible to gain a competitive advantage by targeting the customer segment where market leaders are not focussing.

Consider tailoring your products or services to meet the market's needs and identify at least one unique selling point so that the customers are interested in starting any meaningful discussion. Additionally, by examining where these companies are selling, you can get a sense of which regions or customer segments are most willing to buy your products and offerings.

The bigger the market size, the more the competition is the generic thumb rule, and hence, you need to prepare differently for the well-served markets compared to under-served markets, where you may not face any significant competition but at the same time the size of the market can be very small.

Distribution Network: Establishing reliable distribution networks is essential for effectively reaching customers in the developed market. As a less-known organisation, do not do Direct Sales in the first few years. Your chances of success are lower in a direct sales approach in the initial few years. Always use the local established partner network, irrespective of their contribution in the initial phase. Your local team should help the partner succeed. Get a respectable installation base first before you think of selling directly.

Meetings in person: If your business needs in-person meetings, having a local representative can significantly enhance the effectiveness of face-to-face meetings and overall sales efforts.

A local representative born and brought up there will likely have a deep understanding of the cultural norms, business etiquette, and language nuances prevalent in their country. This understanding can facilitate smoother communication and build rapport with potential clients or partners during face-to-face meetings. They can navigate cultural sensitivities and adapt their communication style to align with local expectations, which can positively impact the outcome of sales negotiations.

Invest in Marketing and Branding: Build brand awareness and credibility through consistent messaging in local trade magazines and participate in local exhibitions where relevant audiences turn up. Your partners must be visible in all such activities, even if you have to finance it to make it happen. This will help you get their committed support to assist you in succeeding in the first phase. Once you are successful, you can change your strategy. Create a website specifically for the local market, catering to their needs, even if that means duplication of work in some cases.

It's essential to research the market in different countries and regions to understand the economic factors that may impact the sales of your products and services.

An organisation had set up its facility in Argentina and was doing good business but could not send the earnings back to India as the local rules stopped it from doing so because of the country's forex policies. Sending US Dollars outside the country was prohibited. So, do your homework before you proceed. Similarly, check the rules for hiring and firing staff, the perks you must pay, and many other things.

Organisations attempt to sell in global markets without visiting those countries. Often, the differences will not be visible when looking at websites and promotional material of competition. You may have to visit the country, meet some customers, and talk to those dealing with competing product lines to learn more about them. Be mentally prepared for surprises, to see that they are either much more developed and advanced than what you thought or much weaker than the impression the documentation gave you. Do not form impressions based on hearsay, which most small and mid-size companies do.

Let's understand how wrong impressions and poor knowledge about competition can impact your ability to make the right decision. In the 1962 Indo-China war, the Indian government did not use the Indian Air Force to push the Chinese army back. The intelligence report based on hearsay assessed that the Chinese Air Force could easily bomb Calcutta, Kanpur, and Madras (now Chennai). There was also a piece of misplaced advice by the then US Ambassador to India, who advised the Indian leadership not to escalate the war by using the Air Force. The result was death, mayhem, and loss of territory by India.

Today, with hindsight, we know that in 1962, the Chinese Air Force had no assets or capability to wage any deep strikes into India across the Himalayas. For this, they would have had to get airborne from Tibetan Airfields at very high altitudes, leading to less weight-carrying capability, implying less fuel, less range, and less weapon load. The IAF had adequate offensive air power and could have defended Indian land and people, and we would not have lost the battle.

So, prepare for your entry into a different geography. Once you have identified the most promising customer segments and regions, you can focus your resources on the areas most likely to give the organisation the best return on investment.

When expanding globally, it's essential to ensure that your products and services comply with local laws and regulations. This might involve obtaining necessary certifications or permits, complying with labelling and packaging requirements, and adhering to local tax laws.

Localising your products and services might involve adjusting product features, packaging, or marketing materials to better appeal to local consumers. For example, you may have to localise the software in Spanish to sell in Latin American countries. The same is true for many other countries. Localisation helps as, unlike in India, the working class does not read or write in English in most non-English-speaking countries. So, when you go to such a country and communicate using English, the message may never reach the intended audience. This will impact business.

A global expansion can be expensive and complex, but if carefully planned and executed, it can lead to significant growth and success.

Travelling globally
Travelling globally for business can be an exciting opportunity to expand your company's reach, build new relationships, and explore new markets. It can, however, also be challenging and complex.

In May 2000, I was moving from Virginia to New Jersey. This was our first family move, and I had organised the tickets. So far, it had been the organisation helping me with all the logistics management. When I reached the airport, I followed the signboards and reached the counter for check-in.

When I showed my ticket, the person at the counter told me I needed to go through a special security check and, hence, had to visit the other counter somewhere inside the airport. I was lost, a bit worried, and had no guidance or help to find that counter for checking in. It was worrying and frustrating. Fortunately, I saw a porter with a big trolley. I asked him for help. With the discussion not progressing, I decided to tip him. I took out a US$20 and gave it to him. Everything else was then taken care of. So do carry some extra cash and be ready for surprises. Some knowledge about local culture always helps.

When your team starts travelling globally, the first few visits will be full of excitement and fear. It makes sense to give them a small checklist to prepare themselves better. Some tips on how to make international business travel more productive:

Plan: Plan your travel itinerary well, including flights, accommodations, and transportation. This will help you to avoid last-minute stress and ensure a smooth journey.

Know your destination: When you plan your travel, do some research on the weather, food, places to stay, the languages people speak, the currency conversion, and anything else which you may need when you reach there. This will make life simpler.

Be prepared for language barriers: Travelling to countries where they speak a different language needs preparation. Have an online translator handy, which you can use to talk to the cab drivers or people in the hotel. Having a local partner to help you is one of the best options. Carry your hotel address written in the local language whenever you leave the hotel. You never know when you might need it.

Eating: Eating in different countries can present several challenges. Different cultures have different attitudes towards food, and what is considered normal or acceptable in one culture may be regarded as strange or offensive in another. This can make knowing what to order or how to eat difficult. People do carry packed food which suits their habits and tastes. In many countries, this can invite penalties if caught at the airport.

In 1999, I was positioned in Virginia, USA. We used to give a bag full of fruits and other eatables to every new joinee, which the person would need to survive the first few days. We started this process since we had heard stories of people from ASEAN countries moving to the USA for the first time and were afraid to step out and buy the basic things needed for survival. Some of them even fainted in their motel or hotel rooms. They all required two to three days to cope with the change. Travelling alone to a new country for the first time can be challenging for many. People are not always very welcoming. So, prepare for it.

Take care of yourself: International travel can be physically and mentally exhausting, so take care of yourself. This might involve getting enough sleep, staying hydrated, and taking breaks to explore the local culture and scenery.

Overall, international business travel can be a challenging but also rewarding experience. Always plan before you travel. Plan your itinerary as much as possible to use your time and resources best.

Organisations often are not sure whether to use travelling salespeople or establish local offices. The reason can be financial expense, convenience, or both. Here are a few points to help you decide.

Opening local office versus travelling salespeople

Opening an office in a new market is advisable if you want a more permanent presence. This can help you build customer relationships, establish local partnerships, and better understand the local business culture. However, opening an office can be expensive, as you may hire local staff and will need to comply with local laws and regulations.

On the other hand, relying on travelling salespeople can be a more cost-effective option, especially if you are testing the waters. Travelling salespeople can help you make connections with potential customers or partners and better understand the market before committing to a more permanent presence.

However, relying solely on travelling salespeople can make building long-term customer relationships and establishing a solid brand presence difficult. Well-served markets prefer to work with organisations with a local office and are reluctant to deal with travelling salespeople until and unless you have a strong partner to represent you, which can be a challenge as big partners with a good presence would like to work with locally established business houses.

If you have the resources, opening an office can be an excellent long-term strategy for building a solid presence in a newly developed market. However, relying on travelling salespeople may be better if you want a more flexible and cost-effective approach.

Along the same lines, the next debate is whether we should hire people locally or send people from our home country.

Hiring local staff versus sending people from your home country

There is no simple answer to this. For example, when we first went to the Thailand market, we saw our predecessors had seen success in that market. So, we started exploring the market. I saw good opportunities to do business. What surprised us was that even though the CIO or the head of Information Technology in the organisation, who could generally speak good English, always recommended our product, the actual users had reservation about it. They could never understand our communication properly. We hired a local staff on a contract basis to help us. However, that did not work as culturally; there is a huge difference between our working styles. We needed updates daily, and they found that very claustrophobic. So, we changed it to a weekly review, and even that proved to be too much for them. They had a much laid-back approach to doing business. Hence, it is important to understand how the local culture works and adapt instead of trying to change it.

Hiring local staff can offer several advantages. They will better understand the local market and culture, which can help you navigate that marketplace better. Secondly, in any geography around the globe, people of the local race, language, and culture are usually more welcome than others.

However, hiring local staff can also present some challenges. For example, finding a team with the right skills and experience can take time, particularly if you are entering a new and unfamiliar market. Additionally, local staff may have different work styles or expectations that can be challenging to manage.

Sending people from your home country can also have advantages. For example, you can ensure that your staff fully aligns with your company's culture, values, and business practices. Additionally, you can ensure that your team has the necessary skills and experience to manage the new operation.

Combining local staff and staff from your home country can be a good approach. This can help you benefit from the advantages of both methods while mitigating some of the challenges. Secondly make them work in the home country with your local team for few months first, to understand things better. This is necessary if your organisation is trying to enter a new market and your intentions are long term.

Create a local ecosystem

A local ecosystem of business partners in a new country is almost mandatory if you want to succeed there.

Market Insights and Understanding: Partners understand the local market, including the business opportunities, competition and regulatory challenges. Their knowledge can help you save valuable time and resources in learning about the new market.

Access to Networks and Relationships: They will have existing relationships and can leverage their relationships to help you reach the relevant audience with minimal loss of time and money. Established local partners can also help you build your credibility much faster.

Navigating Cultural and Linguistic Barriers: The biggest challenge in working in a new country is navigating the cultural nuances and managing the language barriers. This means a lack of free flow of communication, which leads to poor business. The customer takes time to understand you and open up. Some do not open up at all.

Operational Support and Logistical Assistance: With local partners around, you can hit the ground running and become operational quickly. So, in simple words, your time to market reduces drastically.

Managing risks: As a new entrant in the market, in some cases, you may not even know about the potential risks until and unless you face them. Hence, a partner with a local presence can guide you and take you through that journey with minimal challenges.

Building an ecosystem of local business partners in a developed market is like taking a loan from the bank when you are a small name. You must prove that you do not need that money. The bank expects you to offer collateral, guarantees, and more if needed. However, you still take a loan from the bank because you know the benefits. You need to do the same to build the partner ecosystem in a developed country. When we were trying to create a partner ecosystem in Australia, every partner wanted to know if we would have a local presence or not. They also wanted to know the marketing expense, which we would be willing to commit to developing that market. Without your local presence, their interest drops, and without a marketing budget, they know that success is a far cry. Hence, they may not align with you.

Partners in a developed market have many options, and they do not see value in working with unknown players, even if the new entrant offers much better terms. Creating a local partner ecosystem makes it easy for one to operate in a new geography.

Need to go after well served market

Selling in a small market with minimal risks is like swimming in a pond. While you catch small fish regularly, you can never have the earnings of the trawler fishing in the sea. This is one big reason why many IT companies from India went after USA and Western European markets.

Well-served or developed markets offer businesses several advantages but also present challenges. First, there is an option to go after a much bigger market size, leading to more revenue growth at a much faster pace.

The rules of engagement in these markets are well-defined and well-managed by the government. Hence, one can focus entirely on the business aspect. For example, getting payments is a big challenge in a less-served market, and so is enforcing the contract one would have signed. You do not have such problems in a developed market.

Secondly, when you have a user base in a developed market, selling in a developing market becomes easier as your credibility as an organisation increases, which helps the sales team. It enhances a company's credibility and brand reputation.

Targeting smaller markets with lower stakes may offer faster entry and lower barriers to competition. However, revenue and growth are usually limited, and the effort involved in doing that business is relatively high. So, depending on your organization's objectives, resources and long-term strategic vision, you can decide when to go after which market.

Leverage the trade department of your local embassy

Leveraging the trade department of an embassy can be a valuable strategy for obtaining information about a new country's local business environment or geography.

The trade department of an embassy can provide information on the local regulatory environment, market trends and opportunities, and key players in the industry. In some cases, they can also facilitate introductions to local business leaders. This is difficult in a developed economy but works well in a less economically developed country.

Spending marketing dollars

Spending marketing dollars to create visibility and product pull is essential to growth in any market, developed or otherwise. Refer the chapter "Make some noise and become visible" to learn more.

Getting footfall in your stall

Ensuring footfall in your stall can be challenging if you are not a known brand. This is more challenging in a developed market, so prepare differently.

Glamour sells. The allure of glamour and luxury has a universal appeal that transcends geographical and cultural boundaries. Irrespective of what you are selling, glamour can be a highly effective marketing tool that drives brand recognition and sales.

Let's take a real-life example of how adding glamour and doing the same thing can greatly impact the outcome. The company's name, *XYZ Ltd*, is fictitious, although the story accurately represents the happenings that the company followed in more than one country.

Now, *XYZ Ltd* was a software firm interested in selling in Australia. They had a local partner named Empire. They participated in two exhibitions in Sydney. The challenge was getting the audience. In a two-day event, they could hardly get twelve to fourteen visitors to their stall when hundreds were in the hall. So, XYZ Ltd changed its strategy when it took a stall and participated in an exhibition in Sydney.

They had a small stall at CeBIT Sydney. Everyone was wearing a T-shirt of a famous brand with *XYZ LTD* written on the back of the T-shirt. They then announced a gift every two hours. They did a lucky draw and gave away a Kindle to the winner. They also hired two models as hostesses. Their job was to get people to the stall and make them fill out the small form for the lucky draw. The winners were announced on the small whiteboard on the side. Soon, people started coming and checking the names of the winners and enquiring about the products. Overall, it was an impressive show, and in three days, around 200 visitors came to the booth enquiring about the products. Getting the right visitors in the stall is the first step towards increasing the visibility of your product and service. The more visible you become; the more selling becomes easier. So, make it count the next time you participate in an exhibition.

Overall, one should succeed if one allocates the right resources, audits each aspect without bias or prejudice, and reworks the strategy if it does not give the desired results. Getting a few beachheads of success can be a strategy in the initial phase; however, to dominate the market or get a bigger pie, you must focus on a market segment and avoid getting swayed by small temptations of easy business elsewhere. Stick to your market segment and stick to your identified set of potential customers.

19
CHAPTER

Stressful Life vs Peaceful Life

In recent years, there has been an alarming increase in people collapsing due to stress-related illnesses. Stress has become a pervasive aspect of modern life, with individuals struggling to balance work, family, and personal responsibilities. As a result, many people are experiencing physical and mental health issues. This impacts their performance and impacts business.

It is not uncommon to hear about individuals in their 40s and 50s collapsing at work or while exercising due to the overwhelming stress they face daily. The fast-paced nature of modern life has made it difficult for people to switch off and take time for themselves, leading to a constant state of stress and exhaustion.

Individuals must learn how to manage their stress levels effectively to avoid the negative health consequences associated with chronic stress. This includes adequate sleep, and practising mindfulness and relaxation techniques.

Organisations can start with their senior management and go down to as many levels as possible to create an environment where they are motivated to engage in healthy walking, jogging and other activities, which helps reduce stress. Organisations can gift smartwatches to the team and conduct regular competitions, which can be simple but will give the needed nudge to develop healthy habits. The aim is to develop a healthy team that contributes to the organisation's growth.

Sales teams often face more challenges managing internal issues than external ones. Hence, instead of chasing growth and fighting competition, they spend more time pleasing people and saving their jobs. This is when many performers start looking for a new job leading to high attrition in the organisation. Although they are not sure about the next organisation where they will go and if they will find the work environment conducive to work, they take a chance and quit and move on to the next job. Unfortunately, this habit of supporting people who are more loyal to the manager than to the organisation is so prevalent in the majority of organisations that a performer remains dissatisfied and unhappy, irrespective of the organisation they go to. Hence, many come back to the same organisation after a few years. Finding a job where merit will be given a chance and one will get the opportunity to contribute is also a big challenge for the working class. Organisations need to think as to why someone takes the risk of venturing into the unknown. It is not always money, even though money is one big factor. The dissatisfaction drives people crazy and makes them quit and go. So, try to understand one big issue of the sales team and attempt to resolve that without introducing many changes so that it looks doable and becomes a reality.

There are many reasons for high stress in salespeople, and one of them is high sales targets, which they do not think can be achieved. It is not necessary that what they think is correct, but you need the functional head to sit down with them and talk about it and help them understand where they can be wrong and how the targets can be achieved. Accepting vulnerability and asking for help from the team to deliver is not a sign of weakness, it is a sign of showing trust and faith in the team.

Salespeople often experience high stress levels due to the pressure to meet challenging sales targets without the needed support. When an organisation expects exponential growth, it needs to ask what has changed to help it achieve that growth. Every input to doing business if remains constant; exponential growth may not be possible. Stress can result without a clear strategy backed by the needed resources to achieve the defined goals.

While eliminating stress may not be possible, taking steps to manage stress and create a peaceful life can help improve our physical, emotional, and mental well-being. This might involve practising relaxation techniques, building supportive relationships, and finding a healthy work-life balance.

Mastering positive thinking takes practice, but the benefits are worth the effort. With regular practice, individuals can manage stress and anxiety much better.

Find a distraction

Finding healthy distractions at work can help maintain productivity and well-being. One can schedule breaks and engage in physical activity like taking a quick walk. You can also rejuvenate your mind by changing your environment, engaging in creative outlets, and socialising with colleagues. To prevent distractions from interfering with work, it is important to set boundaries and limit them. Balancing work and healthy distractions can improve your overall productivity and enjoyment of daily tasks.

Seek support

Remember, taking care of your employee's mental well-being is essential. With practice and support, one can learn to stay calm, even in difficult situations. Organise such sessions once in a while. This will help break the monotony and will mean more healthy employees who can contribute much more towards the organisation's growth.

Have a tie-up with a third party who offers counselling support. Let the employees talk to these third-party counsellors without completely disclosing their identity. Guarantee secrecy and let no one get punished for talking to the counsellors. Even schools have such counsellors nowadays, so why not professional organisations?

Excessive stress in sales or senior leadership can harm a business in several ways. Stress can hurt business.

Decreased productivity

Sales and senior leadership are often responsible for driving revenue and making critical business decisions. If they are stressed, they may not be able to perform at their best, resulting in decreased productivity.

Change of job profile or job rotation for those who are enthusiastic and willing to take up new challenges is one good way of re-energising the leadership and making them think and act differently, as the new job profile may need a different way of looking at the business.

Do not be surprised if you find that this basic level change on a regular basis resolve many of the organisation's problems.

One basic reason for decreased job satisfaction is not being able to fully utilize one's capabilities and skills in business. When employees contribute less than they could, they feel dissatisfied and stop taking new initiatives.

Decreased creativity and innovation

Stress in leadership is also an outcome of insecurity. An insecure mind impacts the thought process and decision-making. Accepting insecurity as part of life can help individuals cope with it much better. This should help them take more inclusive steps and create a positive environment in the organisation, as they know the fear they harbour will only increase when they do not accept it.

In addition, understanding that insecurity is a normal part of the human experience can also help to reduce stress. It can help leaders realise that they are not alone in their struggles and that others have overcome similar challenges.

Accepting insecurity can help them develop a more positive and resilient mindset and navigate leadership challenges more quickly and confidently.

Sales are indeed crucial for the success of any business. However, it is equally important to remember that humans are not machines and cannot keep pushing themselves indefinitely. Find less forceful ways to engage the teams and drive more business. For example, give merit a chance in the growth of individuals and advocate ethical selling supported by systems and processes. This should help the organisation grow without killing yourself of stress and have happier customers and employees.

Annexure

Here are a couple of articles to help understand why ensuring the growth of small and medium-sized businesses is very essential for the growth of any developing economy like India.

1. 'The Changing Face of SMEs: Here's what to expect' by Samir Sathe, *The Economic Times*, November 20, 2021https://economictimes.indiatimes.com/small-biz/sme-sector/the-changing-face-of-smes-heres-what-to-expect/articleshow/87812380.cms

2. 'MSMEs will be critical sector for pushing India's growth in next 25 years; here's why' by Rajat Mishra, *Business Today*, February 19, 2023 https://www.businesstoday.in/magazine/economy/story/msmes-will-be-critical-sector-for-pushing-indias-growth-in-next-25-years-heres-why-369004-2023-02-05

3. https://www.computerweekly.com/news/252440761/Red-Hat-teams-up-with-Microsoft-in-hybrid-cloud-container-push

Acknowledgements

This book has been possible with the help of individuals I have had the opportunity to watch and be inspired by. Without the experience and support of my peers, this endeavour would not have been a reality. I especially want to thank the individuals that have made a mark on this journey.

1. Sanjeev Mukherjee – Former Global Procurement Head, and Country Manager, Bangladesh & Zambia, *Tata International Limited*
2. TS Varadarajan – Promoter Director with the experience of running multiple organisations.
3. Biswarup Mukherjee – Executive Director (Canadian MNC) and my neighbour.
4. Dr Sameek Bhattacharjee – Professor and Head, Department of Plastic and Reconstructive Surgery, *Atal Bihari Vajpayee Institute of Medical Sciences* and *RML Hospital*, New Delhi
5. Pankaj Chatterjee – Former CTO, *Vayam Technologies*, and currently with a Global System Integrator managing global delivery projects.
6. Jayant Upadhyay – Former Country Manager (UK), *Ramco*, Strategic Sales Industrial Sector (India & South Asia), *IBM*
7. Manomoy Das – Digital Transformation Executive helping startups, and former *IBM* executive.

About the Author

Manojit Majumdar is a sales veteran with a career spanning more than three decades and has attempted to run his own business too. He has travelled across forty countries while selling and forming partnerships. He has worked in multiple organisations, including *IBM* as Country Manager (Small Deals), and is currently working for *Newgen Software Technologies*, responsible for setting up a channel partner network across seventy countries.

This is the second book by the author. His first book, *Lamb Leading Lions: Why we do not have a Google or Microsoft from India*, reigned on the second spot of the *Amazon* bestsellers list under the business section.

Manojit lives in New Delhi with his family. Apart from sales, he is passionate about travelling.

www.ingramcontent.com/pod-product-compliance
Lightning Source LLC
Chambersburg PA
CBHW072147290526
45794CB00004B/1440